25 TOP ROCK SONGS

MW01260048

TAB+ = TAB + TONE + TECHNIQUE

This is not your typical guitar tab book. In the new *Tab+* series from Hal Leonard, we provide you guidance on how to capture the guitar tones for each song as well as tips and advice on the techniques used to play the songs.

Where possible, we've confirmed the gear used on the original recordings via new and previously published interviews with the guitarists, producers, and/or engineers. Then we make general recommendations on how to achieve a similar tone, based on that info.

Some of the songs herein will be easy to play even for advanced beginner players, whereas others present a much greater challenge. In either case, we've identified key techniques in each song that should help you learn the song with greater ease.

ISBN 978-1-4768-1334-9

HAL•LEONARD®
CORPORATION
7777 W. BLUEMOUND RD. P.O. BOX 13819 MILWAUKEE, WI 53213

Visit Hal Leonard Online at
www.halleonard.com

25 TOP HARD ROCK SONGS

Performance Notes 4

Back in Black. 16
AC/DC

Best of Both Worlds 23
VAN HALEN

Crazy Train 35
OZZY OSBOURNE

Detroit Rock City 42
KISS

Doctor, Doctor 53
UFO

Fire Woman. 60
THE CULT

Hair of the Dog 72
NAZARETH

In My Dreams 77
DOKKEN

In-a-Gadda-da-Vida 84
IRON BUTTERFLY

Jailbreak. 88
THIN LIZZY

Nobody's Fool. 93
CINDERELLA

Paranoid 100
BLACK SABBATH

Rock Candy. 104
MONTROSE

Rock of Ages. 117
DEF LEPPARD

School's Out 123
ALICE COOPER

Shout at the Devil 133
MÖTLEY CRÜE

Smoke on the Water 140
DEEP PURPLE

Still of the Night. 145
WHITESNAKE

Stone Cold 162
RAINBOW

Welcome to the Jungle 172
GUNS N' ROSES

Whole Lotta Love. 194
LED ZEPPELIN

Working Man 204
RUSH

You've Got Another Thing Comin' 219
JUDAS PRIEST

Youth Gone Wild 226
SKID ROW

The Zoo 235
SCORPIONS

Guitar Notation Legend 244

PERFORMANCE NOTES TAB. TONE. TECHNIQUE.
By Michael Mueller

"BACK IN BLACK"
AC/DC

After the devastating loss of founding singer Bon Scott in 1980, brothers Angus and Malcolm Young recruited new vocalist Brian Johnson and proceeded to record a tribute to their friend and arguably one of the top 5 hard rock albums of all time: *Back in Black*. The album's title track is featured here.

TONE
It doesn't get much simpler than AC/DC when it comes to guitar tone: a 1968 Gibson SG (Angus) and early 1960s Gretsch Jet with a lone bridge-position FilterTron humbucker (Malcolm) → guitar cable → Marshall (JTM-45) stack. Similarly, you'll want to use a bridge humbucker-equipped axe straight into the distortion channel of a tube amp, or use a good distortion (not metal) pedal.

TECHNIQUE
"Back in Black" is downright epic in its simplicity. Still, there are little quirks you should be aware of when playing the tune. The descending E minor pentatonic lick in the main riff—which was written by Malcolm but played by Angus, because, well, Angus says, "I've got to have the cool bit!"—begins on the second 16th-note subdvision of beat 3, not the downbeat. It's essential you don't rush it! Also in the main riff, the chromatic bass line played against a 5th-string B pedal must be played on the 6th string—even the unison B at the end. This pedal-point idea is recalled in the Interlude as well. Use your pinky finger to fret the A, B♭, and B notes on frets 5, 6, and 7, respectively, and don't be afraid to perform a slight shift for each one rather than relying solely on a stretch.

Angus has one of the best and tastiest vibrato techniques in rock guitar history. It's a fairly fast "wiggle," as he calls it, that's as consistent as the sun rising in the east. Similarly, his frequent string bends are *always* spot-on in-tune. If you can nail these two techniques, you'll be well on your way to credibly copping his largely minor pentatonic lines.

Finally, note the oblique bends at the 22nd fret in the Outro Solo. Here's where having an SG, with its slim neck heel, will come in quite handy. Hitting these on a Les Paul is quite a challenge, especially if you've got beefy fingers.

"BEST OF BOTH WORLDS"
Van Halen

The so-called "Van Hagar" years have been maligned by many, yet Van Halen, with Sammy Hagar at the mic, produced several all-time classic hard rock tracks, including "Best of Both Worlds," from the band's 1986 release *5150*.

TONE
Caveat: Eddie Van Halen has *always* been coy about his guitar tone—even to the point of lying in interviews—so this is largely educated guesswork based on various interviews. By the time Van Halen started the *5150* sessions, Ed was using his Kramer 5150 "Frankenstrat" featuring the banana headstock for live shows, but it's been reported that he did *not* use it in the studio, instead going with his old familiar Frankenstrat through his trusty Marshall Super Lead Plexi. The "chorus" sound comes from an Eventide rack processor. Ed runs two cabs—one dry and one wet (only effects). The effected signal has a slight detune and delay, which when combined with the dry signal, creates a "chorus" effect.

A "super-Strat" with a bridge-position humbucker plugged into a high-gain tube amp with a slight chorus in between will get you there. Also key to the tone in this tune is skillful manipulation of your guitar's volume knob. You'll roll off the volume to "clean" up the signal for the quiet parts, then roll it back to 10 for the full-on dirt.

TECHNIQUE
For the opening riff, fret an open D5 chord using your thumb to fret the low F♯, then fret the G5 chord using your middle finger on the low G and your ring finger on the 2nd-fret D. At bar 5, try using your pick hand's middle, ring, and pinky fingers to pluck the triads on strings 4–2, using your pick to strike the open A when it comes in.

At the solo, the "whiney horse" is sounded with a screaming pinch harmonic quickly bent up a full step then the note is shaken with the whammy bar while simultaneously depressing it—a classic EVH move. The main motif of the solo is another EVH trademark: tapping onto bent notes. While it's important to bend in tune, giving the move a slight "wobble" will both give it some endearing Eddie-ism and help keep it from sounding stiff.

"CRAZY TRAIN"
Ozzy Osbourne

Sometimes it seems as if Randy Rhoads appeared out of nowhere and tragically disappeared by the time guitarists picked their jaws up off the floor. With two albums in under two years, Rhoads had an immeasurable impact on heavy metal guitar, due in large part to his eye-opening fretwork on such Ozzy Osbourne classics as "I Don't Know," "Flying High Again," and the song included here, "Crazy Train."

TONE

His 1970s Gibson Les Paul Custom was Rhoads's weapon of choice for this track. He plugged into a Marshall JMP Super Lead Plexi with Marshall 4x12 cabs loaded with Altec speakers, for a brighter sound. His effects included a variety of MXR pedals (Distortion+, Stereo Flanger, Stereo Chorus, Analog Delay), Korg and Roland tape echoes, a Crybaby wah pedal, and his secret weapon: an MXR 10-band EQ pedal. Further, Rhoads triple-tracked his solo, giving it an even fatter sound on record.

To cop this sound, you'll need an axe with a bridge-position humbucker, preferably a Les Paul–style guitar. Plug it into a high-gain distortion pedal, like the MXR Distortion+, and a chorus pedal to fatten the tone (not a "swirly" chorus, though). The 10-band EQ is actually quite key to Rhoads's tone, if you can swing it. Otherwise, keep your bass low, a good mid-boost, and fairly neutral treble for EQ.

TECHNIQUE

"Crazy Train" features just about every famous Rhoads technique there is: pedal-point riffing, tapping, lightning-fast legato runs, blues-based licks, pull-offs to open strings. Here are a few key points. For the chromatically ascending arpeggio verse fill on the top two strings in the second Chorus, Rhoads admitted in a 1982 interview that it's a bit of a "fake" lick. Which means as long as you start with the F#m arpeggio and climb chromatically for two bars, you're golden—don't worry about hitting exact notes from the transcription when covering the tune. In fact, he said the same about the legato run that caps the solo, that he starts it on D# but never did recall exactly how he played it on record. Still, it's a great exercise to learn that run, as it uses fairly stock hard rock/metal legato patterns. For the harmonic "dips," bend the neck on the Les Paul by simultaneously pushing the top bout into your body while pushing the neck near the headstock away from you. Do so gently, though, so you don't snap it!

"DETROIT ROCK CITY"
Kiss

"Detroit Rock City" is a tribute both to a fan who was killed on his way to a Kiss concert in Charlotte, NC in April 1975, and to the city itself. Producer Bob Ezrin not only wrote and recorded the "news" script and car sounds that open the tune but also wrote the song's famous Guitar Solo/Interlude for Ace Frehley to play.

TONE

Guitarist Ace Frehley used his tobacco-burst Les Paul Standard on early Kiss recordings, played through either a Marshall Super Lead (with 6550 tubes, rather than EL-34s) or a vintage Fender tweed amp, adding an Electro-Harmonix Big Muff for extra hair when needed. In a 1997 interview with *Vintage Guitar*, Paul Stanley says he used a 1967 Gibson EDS-1275 sunburst double-neck guitar for "Detroit Rock City," later confirming that indeed Marshalls and "a Fender or two" were used for amplification.

The obvious approach here is the classic Les Paul through a Marshall. You'll certainly want to use a bridge-position humbucker through a distorted amp, but keep the gain levels moderate, for a more natural distortion than a metal sound.

TECHNIQUE

Producer Bob Ezrin made the most of using guitar layers on "Detroit Rock City." Since the song is quite easy to play from a "technique" standpoint, we're going to focus on how best to approach playing its myriad parts as a lone guitarist. For the first nine bars, follow Gtr. 1. At bar 10, switch to Gtr. 2. At the verses, go back to Gtr. 1, then back to Gtr. 2 at the Chorus. Play the Gtr. 2 part at the first Interlude, but for the second, more famous Interlude (which at one point has *four* harmonized guitars), follow Gtr. 3 if you must play it yourself. You can also try playing the octaves, though it won't sound quite the same. If you've got a harmonizer pedal, set it for a diatonic 3rd above the melody line and kick it in at bar 12 of the Interlude.

Alternatively, try starting with the Gtr. 3 part and at bar 12, switch to Gtr. 5 (a 3rd above Gtr. 3). Then at bar 20, switch to the Gtr. 6 part and stay with it until the end of the section, where you'll need to borrow the 14th-fret C# in place of the rest in that final quarter-note triplet before hitting the C#5 chord on the downbeat of the Verse.

"DOCTOR, DOCTOR"
UFO

One of the all-time underrated guitar heroes, Michael Schenker is nonetheless one of the instrument's greatest rock icons. From his work with brother Rudolf in the Scorpions to his career-defining playing in UFO to the Michael Schenker Group, Schenker's proto-shred guitar style both inspired and informed many of the '80s greatest guitar icons.

TONE

In a recent interview with *Vintage Guitar*, Schenker described his UFO-era rig as a Gibson Flying V, plugged into a wah pedal (either Dunlop or Vox—he used both), then right into a 50-watt Marshall plexi that "was probably set with everything on 10." He further elaborated that he'd sweep through the range of the wah pedal until he found a tone he liked, and then he'd leave it there in the "sweet spot."

Plug a humbucker-equipped axe into a British-style tube amp, and you're pretty much there. If you've got a wah pedal, try the same technique that Schenker uses, trying to match his tones on the UFO records. He does use a flanger on a pick scrape, but it's such a minor thing that if you don't have a flanger, don't worry about it.

TECHNIQUE

At the end of the harmonized guitar part in the Interlude, you'll come across oblique bends played in a quarter-note triplet rhythm. Even though you're holding the first bend, make sure the notes don't ring together. You might even want to use slides instead of bends here, as Schenker often did in live settings. To do so, strike the note that is to be bent, but instead of bending, slide it up two frets. In both cases, fret that note with your middle finger.

On a related note, Schenker uses quite a few quarter-note triplets in this tune. This rhythm is often a sticking point for all sorts of musicians. In 4/4 time, a quarter-note triplet is a triplet played over a half note. In essence, if you break those two beats of the half note into the more familiar eighth-note triplet, and then play *every other* subdivision, you're playing a quarter-note triplet: *trip*-uh-*let*, trip-*uh*-let.

"FIRE WOMAN"
The Cult

Like Michael Schenker in the 1970s, the Cult's Billy Duffy not only was one of the most underrated guitarists of the 1980s but also had one of the most straightforward balls-to-the-wall rock guitar tones of an era rife with over-processing. "Fire Woman," from the band's 1989 Top 10 album *Sonic Temple*, encapsulates much of Duffy's signature style.

TONE

Though he's probably best known as a devotee of the Gretsch White Falcon, Duffy used an early 1970s Gibson Les Paul Custom for this track, plugged into a Harry Kolbe–modded Marshall 2210 cranked for power-tube distortion. He also used a phaser on this track as well as two delays—one set for eighth-note regeneration and the other for quarter-note regeneration, with two repeats.

A Les Paul or humbucker-equipped guitar through a distorted tube amp is your tonal base. Set your phaser for a very slow rate and not much depth. If you have two delay pedals, follow the instructions above. With a tempo of 132 bpm, quarter-note repeats will be at 454 ms, and eighth-note repeats at 227 ms. If you only have one delay pedal, try each and choose the one you prefer.

TECHNIQUE

The arpeggiated opener is the first of several signature riffs in "Fire Woman." The second is the melody that slides up and down the 3rd string. Here, use either your index or middle finger on the slides—whichever is more comfortable. The first "tricky" part comes in at the Pre-Chorus, where D5, F5, and G5 power chords are played in arpeggio fashion and embellished with 16th-note triplet licks. The key to this section is to lead to the next chord change, which occurs on the "and" of beat 4 in each bar, with your index finger, for the easiest transition. Your pinky finger will also need to be up to task for the hammers and pulls on the F5 and G5 chords.

One of Duffy's rock guitar heroes is Angus Young, evident in the simplicity of both his guitar tone and his soloing approach. The solos here are largely in D minor pentatonic and feature a *lot* of bends—particularly in the Outro. Like Duffy and Young, you'll want to make you own those bends, nailing the target pitches throughout.

"HAIR OF THE DOG"

Nazareth

"Hair of the Dog," the title track from Nazareth's 1975 breakout (in the U.S.) album, is often mistakenly called "Son of a Bitch," both due to the repeated phrase that serves as the lyrical hook and because the title never appears in the lyrics. More to our point, though, the tune features an all-time classic guitar riff in E courtesy of guitarist Manny Charlton. Let's take a look.

TONE

Like so many 1970s rockers, Charlton was a Les Paul into a Marshall guy, specifically a Les Paul Custom into a 1971 Marshall 100-watt Super Lead, with a Sola Sound Fuzz Box providing the "hair," so to speak. This track also features a talk-box and a wah pedal.

Likewise, you'll want to use a humbucker-equipped guitar like a Les Paul or SG through a moderately distorted tube amp. Use a fuzz pedal for the talk box section. As most of you won't have a talk box, however, you can instead play that section with the wah pedal—toe down for the 7th-fret E and toe up for the low E.

TECHNIQUE

The main riff of the song, which derives quite obviously from the Beatles' "Day Tripper," is pretty simple, though you'll need to execute those bluesy bends on the 5th-fret G note with your pinky, so if you're not used to using your pinky in this manner, give it some practice.

In the Coda, you'll note some 16th-note, clean-toned D major dyads. Unless you're playing this tune in a band with a second guitarist, you can just ignore these.

"IN MY DREAMS"

Dokken

Of all the hair metal–era guitar heroes, Dokken's George Lynch reigns supreme. In a 2007 feature in *Guitar Edge*, '80s icons like Reb Beach, Phil Collen, and Vivian Campbell all named Lynch as their favorite guitarist of the era! "In My Dreams," from Dokken's 1985 breakout album *Under Lock and Key*, showcases both Lynch's riffing and soloing brilliance.

TONE

Whereas the '80s was filled with the excesses of highly processed guitar sounds, Lynch's rig was classic by comparison. In the studio, Lynch most often relied on his pre-ESP custom "Tiger" super-Strat guitar loaded with a Duncan SH-6 Distortion humbucker. According to producer Neil Kernon, Lynch used a Marshall that was heavily modified by Lee Jackson for these sessions, with an original square-button Ibanez TS-808 Tube Screamer providing the boost. Michael Wagener, who also was a producer on that album, recalls an additional Marshall as well as two Laney amps, cabs in three different rooms and an insane number of mics to capture it all, plus the secret weapon: running the final signal through a Fostex 4-track recorder!

To best capture Lynch's tone, use a humbucker-equipped super-Strat plugged into a high-gain tube amp. A Tube Screamer or similar overdrive pedal for extra mid boost and gain on the solo is a must!

TECHNIQUE

That ringing arpeggio heard the second time through the main riff is pretty important, and the good news is you can combine the parts to pull it off alone. When you get to that point, your bassist will be playing the B–D–E line that approaches each chord, so you can focus on the arpeggios in bars 6–7, before switching back to the power chords.

The highlight of the solo is the long legato section in which Lynch executes a remarkable left-hand stretch, anchoring his index finger at the 12th fret, using his middle finger on the 15th fret, and alternating between the 19th and 20th frets with his pinky. In witness of its difficulty, you'll see Lynch almost always hoist his guitar higher or rest it on his knee to pull this off. Alternatively, you can *tap* the notes on the 19th and 20th frets using your pick hand's middle finger. It might not look as cool, but it's a *lot* easier.

"IN-A-GADDA-DA-VIDA"

Iron Butterfly

Iron Butterfly's 1968 release *In-a-Gadda-da-Vida* is regarded in many circles as the first "heavy metal" album, pre-dating Black Sabbath's debut by two years. It was also the first heavy rock album to receive extensive airplay and in fact received the very first, albeit unofficial (pre-RIAA), *platinum* sales award, bestowed by the late, great Ahmet Ertegun, who was the head of Atco Records at the time. The title track is a 17-minute magnum opus, but here we present the 2:53 single version.

TONE

Fuzz tone, baby! Seventeen-year-old guitarist Erik Brann (aka, Braun or Braunn), who reportedly had been playing guitar for only three months when this song was recorded, ran a Mosrite guitar through a Mosrite Fuzzrite pedal and into a Vox Super Beatle. Although this is certainly an odd combination for what is one of the earliest "heavy metal" recordings of all time, there's no denying that Braun created a rather powerful and unique sound.

Although you can't get this tone with just any fuzz pedal, most people will not want to spend money to track down an old Fuzzrite or the boutique copies out there. You'll be able to approximate the tone using the classic Les Paul–Marshall setup, with a Fuzz Face or Way Huge Swollen Pickle fuzz in between.

TECHNIQUE

While playing through the transcription, I noticed that I was occasionally playing those opening quarter-note Ds in staccato fashion, when in fact they are ringing notes, so watch out for that pitfall. Begin the riff in 2nd position, with your pinky finger on the 5th-fret D. When moving up to the 7th-fret A on the 4th string, try using your pinky finger, then your ring finger on Ab, middle finger on G and on the slide down to F, which then puts you back in 2nd position to repeat the riff.

"JAILBREAK"
Thin Lizzy

Some would say that Thin Lizzy guitarists Brian Robertson and Scott Gorham essentially invented the "twin guitar attack" that would later be popularized by such New Wave of British Heavy Metal bands like Judas Priest, Iron Maiden, and Def Leppard. Although "Jailbreak" doesn't feature these twin harmonies, it's nonetheless a high point in the band's catalog and an all-time rock classic.

TONE

Although Robertson typically played Marshalls, he plugged his 1973 Gibson Les Paul Deluxe into a Carlsbro combo amp along with a Colorsound wah pedal for the *Jailbreak* sessions. Similarly, Gorham also used a Les Paul Deluxe, outfitted with mini-humbuckers, and played through 100-watt Marshall amps.

The Thin Lizzy guitar sound is almost the prototypical Les Paul through a Marshall sound, so that's your best bet for copping the tone. You'll certainly want a humbucking bridge pickup through a moderately distorted amp. You'll also need a wah pedal such as a Crybaby, Morley, or Vox.

TECHNIQUE

In the Interlude, use your fret hand's middle finger to fret the 7th-fret E on the 5th string. From there, you can either assign one fret per finger for the four notes on the 4th string, which will require you to "roll" your middle finger down to the A and back to the E again, or you can use your ring finger on both the 7th and 8th frets of the 4th string.

Also in this section, there are police sirens wailing in the background. You can mimic this live if you've got a whammy-equipped axe by divebombing open strings and natural harmonics. You can also manipulate the whammy bar while alternately plucking an E/B dyad on the top two strings at the 12th fret, to emulate a European-style siren.

"NOBODY'S FOOL"
Cinderella

Whereas the hair metal era was largely defined by over-the-top, flashy guitar playing, it also produced many of the greatest power ballads of all time, including Cinderella's "Nobody's Fool." Here, guitarists Tom Keifer and Jeff LaBar's "feel and fire" approach takes the song to soaring heights.

TONE

In the era of pointy-headstock guitars and refrigerator racks filled with digital preamps and effects, Cinderella went with a much more organic tone, courtesy of Keifer's love for vintage gear. Armed with a Gibson Les Paul and a Marshall plexi, Keifer swam against the tide to an ocean of great tone. LaBar, at the time, used a humbucker-equipped Charvel super-Strat with a Floyd Rose, but is also a fan of vintage axes. You can especially hear the difference in the solo, where Keifer plays the first four bars, LaBar the next three, and then final two harmonized bars.

Although LaBar uses his whammy bar once in the solo, you can easily play the tune using just a Les Paul or similar axe, which offers overall a better tonal representation. Plug into a distorted British-style tube amp with the gain about half way.

TECHNIQUE

For the opening arpeggio riff, begin by fretting an open Am shape. When you reach the Dm/A on beat 3, place your pinky finger on the 3rd-fret D and shift your index finger over to the 1st-fret F, then back to the Am shape in bar 2. At bar 4, use your ring finger for the 3rd-fret C on string 5, for the easiest transition.

Both Guitar Solos are highly melodic ones in A natural minor. LaBar very effectively uses volume swells in the first 4-bar salvo. Strike each fretted note in the first two bars with your volume off, then gradually but somewhat rapidly turn your volume knob all the way up.

In the second solo, bar 5, rather than sliding down to the 3rd-fret D and then having to quickly move back up to 5th position, you might instead want to play that D on the 3rd string at the 7th fret, thus keeping you in position for the next bar.

"PARANOID"
Black Sabbath

If Iron Butterfly's psychedelic acid rock constituted the *first* heavy metal band, Black Sabbath's dark, macabre riffs represented its coming of age with Sabbath's 1970 release *Paranoid* perfecting the form. As opposed to the typically sludgy tempos, the album's title track is an uptempo whirlwind of power chords and pentatonics, courtesy of the grandfather of heavy metal guitar, Tony Iommi.

TONE

Iommi gets his classic Sabbath tone from a 1965 Gibson SG Special with a P-90 pickup in the bridge and a custom-wound John Birch Simplux P-90–style single coil in the neck position. The SG is plugged into a Laney Supergroup amp (all controls on "10") through Laney 4x12 cabs loaded with 25-watt Goodman speakers. He also placed a Dallas Arbiter Rangemaster Treble Boost in line. The Orange amps famously seen in the "Paranoid" video were just for the shoot.

A P-90–equipped axe is ideal, though a Les Paul–type with humbuckers will also suffice. Plug that into a British-style tube amp like a Laney, Orange, or Marshall, but avoid any highly saturated "modern" metal tones. With today's amps, you won't need a treble boost.

TECHNIQUE

For the Intro, some players prefer to play an open low E, for an even more "sludgy" sound. The 6th-string rooted power chords and barre chords are a must for achieving the Sabbath sound, plus they facilitate that super-cool Em7 chord stab at the end of the main riff!

The Outro Solo is pretty straightforward E minor pentatonic material, but the opening 1-1/2 step prebend can be a tricky proposition. To get a feel for just how far you've got to push the 3rd string, first sound the G at the 12th fret, then slide down and bend the E using your ring finger, along with your middle and index fingers for support, until it reaches the G pitch. Do this a few times, until it's ingrained in your "muscle memory." Given that it's the first note of the solo, you really don't want to be flat.

"ROCK CANDY"
Montrose

The 1973 self-titled debut of Montrose, featuring guitarist Ronnie Montrose and singer Sammy Hagar, is one of the most important records in rock guitar history for its HUGE sound. The album was produced by Ted Templeman and engineered by Don Landee—the same duo who would later work on Van Halen's first six albums. "Rock Candy" is one of the highlights of that record and features one of rock's greatest riffs.

TONE

Montrose achieved this timeless tone using a Gibson Les Paul through a Fender Bandmaster 3x10 combo he purchased at a garage sale for $90 the day before he entered the studio to record the album. He reportedly also used a Big Muff distortion pedal during these sessions. Prior to his death in March 2012, Montrose had been using Baker B3 guitars through Bogner Shiva amps, stating in interviews that he felt those amps were what came closest to the classic Montrose tone.

Similarly, you'll want to use a Les Paul or other humbucker-equipped guitar through a powerful tube amp such as a Bogner or a Marshall. With a master volume amp, you shouldn't need a Big Muff or other distortion pedal in line.

TECHNIQUE

The classic E blues riff is played in open position, and you'll likely be familiar with these now-stock licks. At the Chorus, Montrose slips in some cool 6ths intervals, á la Jimmy Page. There are two ways to approach these: Because you're starting from an A5 likely fretted with an index-finger barre, the logical move is to fret the A6sus4 with your middle finger on the D and your ring finger on the F♯, then slide your ring finger up to G for the A7, with your pinky grabbing the 5th-fret

E. Alternatively, you can play that D/F♯ interval with your index/middle finger, respectively, sliding your middle finger to G and grabbing the E with your ring finger. Choose the one most comfortable to you.

The other key technique to note in this tune is the plethora of unison bends. Montrose nails these with flawless pitch, and so should you strive to do the same. For all of these bends, your index finger frets the higher string and your ring finger frets the note to be bent.

"ROCK OF AGES"
Def Leppard

Looking back at the 1980s, there can be little doubt that Def Leppard absolutely ruled the roost, with their albums *Pyromania* and *Hysteria* consecutively selling over 10 million copies each. Even now, nearly 30 years later, the band sells out arenas and amphitheaters the world over. Their smash hit featured here, "Rock of Ages," truly lives up to its name.

TONE
It was during the recording of *Pyromania* that guitarist Pete Willis was fired and new guitarist Phil Collen brought on board. Still, Collen recalls those sessions and filled us in. Willis and Steve Clark recorded the rhythm parts using primarily Fender Strats and Teles through Marshall heads and a "well-mic'd" Marshall cab. When Collen came in, he ran his own 50-watt Marshall through that same cab and used his black, triple-pickup Ibanez Destroyer—the same one seen in the music video—to record the solo.

A Fender Tele through a Marshall will nail the rhythm tone for you, but you'll need a whammy-equipped guitar for the solo, so a super-Strat may be your best choice here. As for amps, a high-gain tube amp like a Marshall is your best bet. Whatever you use, keep the gain down to AC/DC levels rather than a highly saturated metal tone.

TECHNIQUE
At the Chorus, a single-note rhythm figure enters roughly outlining C, Em, and A chords. For the Em and A versions, it's clear that you'll use your pinky, ring, and index fingers to fret the G, F♯, and E notes, respectively. For the opening C, however, you can either fret the 5th-string C pedal tone with your middle finger and play the aforementioned notes as described, or you can fret that C with your index finger and use your ring and middle fingers on the G and F♯ notes, respectively, and then shift back one fret to play the E with your index as well. Although this approach is not as efficient, some guitarists will feel more comfortable fretting that root C with the index finger.

In the solo, Collen executes several full-step bends with his fret hand's index finger—a favorite device of Jeff Beck as well. You'll need to pull the string down, toward the floor, so apply a good amount of string pressure and rotate your wrist away from the neck to help properly execute these bends.

"SCHOOL'S OUT"
Alice Cooper

Alice Cooper has worked with quite a few guitarists through the years, but few compare to the original duo of Glen Buxton and Michael Bruce. Buxton, who was considered the lead guitarist, co-wrote "School's Out" with Cooper and is the man responsible for the tune's signature riff.

TONE
Buxton famously employed a 1960s Gibson Les Paul SG Custom, with a three-humbucking-pickup configuration and a Bigsby B-5 tremolo. Bruce similarly played SGs loaded with P-90 soapbars. Both ran their guitars through Marshall heads, though Buxton also had begun to use Fender amps beginning around the *School's Out* sessions, and the tone on this main riff could certainly be the result of a cranked tweed, possibly through 10" speakers.

Likewise, a humbucker-equipped Les Paul or SG is your ticket to summer vacation. If you can crank a Fender or Marshall to natural breakup, give it a shot. Otherwise, try an overdrive or distortion pedal but with the gain only around 6.

TECHNIQUE
If you're playing this tune as the lone guitarist, follow the Gtr. 1 part, switching to the fills and lead licks of Gtr. 3 at every opportunity. If you don't have a keyboard player, you'll also want to take on Gtr. 4 part in the Bridge.

If you *do* have a keyboardist or second guitarist, and you find yourself having to produce the feedback behind the keyboard part, you're going to need a lot of volume and be in very close proximity to your speakers. Point your guitar's body/pickups toward the speaker(s), and slowly move it around until you find the "sweet spot," where the feedback takes hold.

"SHOUT AT THE DEVIL"
Mötley Crüe

Mötley Crüe's 1983 release, *Shout at the Devil*, would also be the notorious sleaze-rock quartet's breakout record. While bassist Nikki Sixx, drummer Tommy Lee, and singer Vince Neil represented the larger-than-life rock-star image for which Crüe has come be known, guitarist Mick Mars has always been the glue that kept the band musically together. "Shout at the Devil" is just one of a career's fill of killer riffs.

TONE

For the last 15 years or so, Mars has gravitated heavily toward Fender Strats, but for Crüe's early days, including "Shout at the Devil," he used a 1972 Gibson Les Paul Custom with PAF humbuckers plugged into a 1971 Marshall modded with a master volume added to the back. He also used an Electro-Harmonix LPB-1 (linear power booster) in line for extra push on the head.

To cop Mick's sinister metal tones here, use a humbucker-equipped guitar plugged into a fairly high-gain amp. You want to set the gain level and EQ to attain a generous amount of gain but with plenty of edge and crunch.

TECHNIQUE

The first thing to note here is the D-standard tuning. With all the open A notes throughout, plus the open E5 power chords in the rhythm guitar part of the solo, there really is no standard-tuning alternative.

Mars's frequent use of unison bends is one of the song's key elements, so you'll want to make sure you can nail these in tune every time. To practice, first strike the stationary note on the B string, then strike the note on the G string and bend up until the pitch matches.

In the Guitar Solo, begin with the unison bends of Gtr. 2, then switch to the Gtr. 1 part for the final two beats of bar 2. Next comes the fun part: switching back to Gtr. 2, Mars pulls of a great whammy bar emulation with his Les Paul by executing a trill between B and D notes at the 12th and 15th frets, respectively, while reaching over with his picking hand, grabbing the B string, and pulling it up and releasing to create the indicated bends. If you're using a whammy-equipped axe, you can just go to the bar, but either way, this is a cool trick to have in your arsenal.

"SMOKE ON THE WATER"
Deep Purple

It's impossible to estimate just how many guitarists cite Deep Purple's "Smoke on the Water" as the first rock riff they ever learned since the tune's 1972 release on *Machine Head*—particularly given the riff's status as one of the top five, if not *the* greatest, in rock history.

TONE

Blackmore plugged his Fender Strat into Marshall Major 200-watt heads with a factory cascade mod, in conjunction with a Hornby-Skewes Treble Booster, to recover the mids and highs lost with the factory mod.

For the most authentic tone, you will definitely want to use a Strat or Strat-style guitar with single-coil pickups in both the bridge and neck positions for this tune. Use the bridge position for the riff, verses, and chorus, and the neck position for the solo. Plug into a British tube amp such as a Marshall or Vox. Unless you actually own one of those rare Majors, you won't need the treble boost.

TECHNIQUE

Based on the timbre of the notes on the original recording, we believe the opening G5 is played on the open G and D strings, as tabbed; however, Blackmore commonly plays this dyad at the 5th fret of the 5th and 4th strings, using a ring-finger barre. This puts him in 3rd position for the whole riff. He also reaches up to the 6th fret for the Db5 dyad with his ring finger and then shifts back to the 5th fret for the C5 dyad. Further, use your thumb and index finger to *pluck* the riff. Blackmore has also been known to play it with a pick, but using all upstrokes, to accentuate the tonic—never play it with all downstrokes, per Blackmore's own advice!

One of the tricky parts in the solo is nailing the pitches when alternating between fretted notes and bent ones, as in measures 5–6 and 17–18. Use your ring finger, reinforced by your index and middle fingers, for these bends. Use those same fingers when executing the famous "gradual release" bend at the 8th fret of the 1st string, in bars 20–22. Although your index finger will be at the 6th fret here, shift back slightly to use your middle finger to make the bend from F to G, at the 6th fret of the 2nd string, that closes the solo.

"STILL OF THE NIGHT"
Whitesnake

When the video for "Still of the Night" hit MTV airwaves in 1987, it immediately propelled the Zeppelin-esque supergroup Whitesnake to the top of the rock charts. Which was cool, except that singer David Coverdale fired the entire band—including John Sykes, the guitarist who wrote and recorded this monster track as well as nearly the entire album—prior to the album's release. As a result, it was left to super-pickers Vivian Campbell and Adrian Vandenberg to fill Sykes's sizable shoes.

TONE
Despite the pointy-headstock Kramer (Campbell) and Fernandes Vandenberg (Vandenberg) super-Strat axes in the video, Sykes relied on his trusty 1978 Gibson Les Paul Custom, with a Gibson "Dirty Fingers" humbucking bridge pickup (since replaced with a PAF). There is speculation that he used a Charvel San Dimas with a Floyd Rose for the overdubbed whammy dives. Normally a Marshall man, Sykes here used two Mesa/Boogie Coliseum heads, which have a Mark III–type preamp section but with six 6L6 power tubes in the power section. For effects, Sykes used Lexicon PCM 41 delays and PCM 70 modulation rack units.

Sykes has one of the beefiest and saturated tones in metal history. As a result, humbucking pickups are absolutely necessary. For amplification, choose a unit with highly saturated gain, like a Boogie Dual Rectifier or Mark IV, or a Peavey 6505. A master volume Marshall or similar amp, in league with an overdrive pedal for solos, will also get you there. Just add a touch of delay, and you're good to go.

TECHNIQUE
For once and for all … Sykes did *not* use a violin bow in the Instrumental section! He does, however, frequently use an open G string in place of the 5th-fret G (4th string) and open B in place of the 4th-fret B (3rd string) when playing this section, which makes for greater economy of motion. Try it both ways to see which works better for you.

There are two approaches to playing the solo in this tune: 1) play it as written, or 2) just shred like crazy in E minor for the first two bars, as Sykes does (and always has done), making sure to hit the notes as written in bars 3–6. I've seen him play this several times, and he *never* plays the same thing twice.

"STONE COLD"
Rainbow

Whereas guitarist Ritchie Blackmore got the spotlight on Deep Purple's "Smoke on the Water" (see page 11), he shows what a great team player he is on this track from Rainbow's 1982 release *Straight Between the Eyes*. But even in this laid-back tune, Blackmore shows in his Outro Solo a few reasons (arpeggios, intervallic lines) why he's the father of neoclassical metal guitar!

TONE
Just like he did with "Smoke on the Water," Blackmore plugged his 1970s Fender Strat (with scalloped fretboard) into incredibly loud, modded Marshall heads and 4x12 cabs.

Grab a Strat or similar single-coil guitar and plug into a Marshall or similar Brit-style tube amp. If you listen closely, you'll notice that Blackmore doesn't play with much gain in this tune, even in the solo. For the Intro and Verse riff, use the neck pickup either through the clean channel, or through the distortion channel set for slight distortion but with your guitar's volume rolled back until it's clean. Then, you can just roll up the volume and switch to the bridge pickup for the Pre-Chorus. For the main and Outro Solos, stomp on an overdrive pedal such as the Ibanez Tube Screamer or BOSS Super-Overdrive, with little gain but a slight level and tone boost.

TECHNIQUE
The tune's main chord progression is Am7–G, and Blackmore very effectively demonstrates how to make a simple harmony sound much cooler using dyads. In bar 9 of the Intro, you're faced with the choice of either sliding up the 4th string with your ring finger to the 10th fret and using your middle finger on the 9th-fret E and pinky on the 10th-fret F, or changing to the likely more comfortable 2nd finger on the 4th string, 10th fret, using your index and middle fingers on E and F, respectively. I prefer the latter, but use whichever feels better for you.
In the Pre-Chorus, you'll see C, G, and D chord partials. From a technique standpoint, you should just fret the entire open chord shape for each, focusing on hitting just the indicated notes. But in doing so, if you *do* hit any extraneous strings, at least they'll be in key.

"WELCOME TO THE JUNGLE"
Guns N' Roses

Just as hair metal was reaching its zenith (figuratively *and* literally), a band of misfits rose up from the gutters of Sunset Strip wielding Les Pauls and Marshalls, instead of pointy-headstock super-Strats and refrigerator racks. With their 1987 debut, *Appetite for Destruction*, Guns N' Roses injected a much-needed dose of grit and danger to the hairspray and spandex scene.

TONE

Izzy used a Gibson ES-125 through a Mesa/Boogie Mark III head and Carvin 4x12 cab. Slash got hold of his now-famous Seymour Duncan–loaded '59 Les Paul copy built by Kris Derrig and plugged it into a rented Marshall Silver Jubilee head (which is the basis for his signature Marshall head).

To cop this classic guitar sound, go with a Les Paul or similar humbucker-equipped axe into a Marshall or similar British-style tube amp. For the delay, use a stompbox like the classic BOSS DD-3 or similar model. Set the delay to a dotted eighth-note regeneration (445 ms, at the tempo of 101 bpm), with two repeats, dial in some reverb, and you're ready to enter the jungle!

TECHNIQUE

As you'll see, there is a *lot* going on in this tune. In the Intro riff, beginning in bar 2, there's a *hemiola*, or *three-against-four*, feel happening, which will help you play the part. You're playing steady 16th notes, but it feels like sets of triplets, so if you break it up that way, it's easier: B–B–B, A–B–A, F♯–B–F♯, E–B–E, and so forth.

The basis for the main Verse riff is rather simple, but you need to execute it with swagger. Pay special attention beginning in Verse 2, where Slash takes a few blues-scale excursions; you *could* just stick with the main riff, but this part is just so cool you won't want to.

For the opening tritones in the first solo, use your index finger in string 4 and middle on string 3; doing so allows you to keep your middle finger planted at the 13th fret for the ensuing 3rds dyad. In bar 5, execute the 19th-fret bend with your ring finger, then on beat 4 either walk that finger back chromatically to the 17th-fret bend, or use your middle finger on the 18th fret following the bend and then move that one back for the 17th-fret bend.

"WHOLE LOTTA LOVE"
Led Zeppelin

While it's debatable to call Led Zeppelin the first "heavy metal" band, there is no doubt that this ear-splitting anthem set the bar for a heavy metal song. Driven by Jimmy Page's powerful one-chord riff, Robert Plant's primordial moans and shrieks, and the pummeling rhythm section of bassist John Paul Jones and drummer John Bonham, "Whole Lotta Love" became the first metal tune to make the Top 10.

TONE

Jimmy Page told *Guitar World* in 1991 that he used his "Les Paul" to record "Whole Lotta Love," but which one? Well, producer Eddie Kramer reportedly said that Page used his Black Beauty (Les Paul Custom) for all of *Led Zeppelin II*. The secret weapons, though, were his Sola Sound Tone Bender Professional MKII distortion pedal (as seen in *It Might Get Loud*) and a Vox UL4120 amp, which has a solid-state preamp and KT88 power tubes. He also used a Vox wah pedal left in the "toe down" position for the solo and a slide in combination with backwards echo for the "answer" to the vocal line "whole lotta love."

The old "Les Paul into a Marshall" adage is a good one for you to follow here. You should be able to drive the amp enough to not need a distortion pedal, but you can add one if necessary. Keep in mind, too, that Page often played his rhythm parts using *both* pickups of his Les Paul; you should definitely give that a shot. As mentioned above, a wah pedal in toe down position is essential for the solo.

TECHNIQUE

The main riff is about straightforward as it gets and is fairly easy to play. One quirky "Page-ism" found here is the doubling of the D note in the riff (5th fret of string 5 and open string 4). This helps thicken the stew, if you will.

The solo—one of the most memorable in rock history—is of the call-and-answer variety, where Page's six monumental blues licks answer staccato E5 power chords. In bar 2, be sure you don't rush the open-position pull-offs; strive for an even rhythm. In bar 4 you'll see a whopping two-step (major 3rd) bend. Use your ring finger to fret the note and reinforce the bend with your middle and index fingers.

"WORKING MAN"

Rush

In early 1974, Rush was just another rock band trying to make their way in Canada, when a DJ named Donna Halper at Cleveland's WMMS decided to spin a new song called "Working Man." The song was an immediate hit with the area's blue-collar working class rock fans, leading to Mercury Records deciding to release the band's self-titled debut in the States. And the rest, as they say, is history.

TONE

In the band's early years, guitarist Alex Lifeson was using a tobacco-burst 1968 Gibson ES-335 through a 50-watt Marshall JMP head and a Marshall 4x12 cab. He also employed a Fuzz Face for that extra bit of "hair" on his tone.

You can use a Les Paul or similar humbucker-equipped guitar here, but an ES-335 or similar semi-hollowbody does make a difference. Plug into a British-type tube amp set for moderate to high gain. If you're using a more modern two-channel or master volume amp, you probably won't need a fuzz pedal, but if you use one, keep it subtle.

TECHNIQUE

For the cool 4ths riff of the Chorus, use your fret hand's index finger to bar strings 5–6 at the 7th fret, using the "rolling" technique as you alternate strings, to keep the notes from ringing over the top of each other. To do so, hold down the 6th string with your fingertip, allowing the fleshy finger pad to mute the 5th string. Then "roll" your finger down to fret the 7th fret of the 5th string with the fleshy pad of your finger while the fingertip mutes the 6th string. In bar 2 you'll slide your finger down to the 5th fret and repeat the process. In bar 3, slide down to the 3rd fret, only this time the harmony switches to 5ths.

Lifeson is an accomplished soloist, but when he plays fast, his lines do tend to be a bit haphazard—something to keep in mind if you get frustrated to learn the solos note-for-note as presented, especially the second one. I don't want to say you can just noodle in E minor pentatonic with the occasional 6th (C♯) and 2nd (F♯), hitting all the highlight notes, but, well, you can. If you're not comfortable playing in all five pentatonic positions, you'll find it *very* helpful to work on them.

"YOU'VE GOT ANOTHER THING COMIN'"

Judas Priest

Thin Lizzy is often credited with the birth of the "twin-guitar attack" in hard rock, but it's Judas Priest's Glenn Tipton and K.K. Downing that set the bar for all hard rock and metal bands to come. Their 1982 album *Screaming for Vengeance*, buoyed by the hit "You've Got Another Thing Comin'," marked the pinnacle of their popularity.

TONE

"You've Got Another Thing Comin'" represents a tonal bridge between the more overdriven sounds of 1970s classic hard rock and the highly processed and saturated tones that followed. Given the 22nd-fret bends in his solo, it's almost certain he used his Gibson SG (stock PAF humbuckers) on this track. He used 50- and 100-watt Marshall plexis along with a JCM 800, into Marshall cabs. Downing favored a Gibson Flying V plugged into Marshalls. Both guitarists had Pete Cornish–built pedalboards with a laundry list of effects. A Roland chorus unit was used on this tune.

You'll certainly want a guitar equipped with a bridge-position humbucker, be it an SG, Flying V, Les Paul, or super-Strat for this tune. A more modern-voiced Marshall-style tube amp is your best bet. You'll want more gain/saturation than, say, a Thin Lizzy or Led Zeppelin tone, but stay away from thrash and modern metal levels. Try about "7" on the gain level of typical Marshall master volume amp. You'll also need a chorus pedal. Set the rate quite low (1–2), the depth around 4–5, and the level around 6–7.

TECHNIQUE

In bar 8 (and 12) of the Intro, where the A/E and B/F♯ dyads are played against the F♯5 pedal, hold down the F♯m7 chord fingering at the 2nd fret, being very careful with your pick attack and using fret-hand muting to separate the dyads—you don't want it to sound like one big "jazzy" F♯m7 chord in a metal classic like this!

The solo is culled almost exclusively from the F♯ minor pentatonic scale, with the ♭5th (C) making an all-important appearance in the signature phrase of bars 5–6. The main thing to watch in this solo is your time and rhythm. Although it may appear as though Tipton is merely shredding on stock F♯ minor pentatonic patterns, he's playing with a great amount of rhythmic precision, very effectively pacing the solo via eighth notes, triplets, and 16ths. Be sure to use a metronome to help maintain rhythmic discipline.

"YOUTH GONE WILD"
Skid Row

Skid Row is sort of the "forgotten" hair band. Toeing the line between glam and gutter, the band's guitarists, Dave "Snake" Sabo and Scotti Hill, crafted huge riffs, while singer Sebastian Bach—owner of the biggest and best pipes of the era—belted out the lyrics with equal power. "Youth Gone Wild" was the first single from the band's self-titled debut.

TONE

Hill used a custom Spector guitar (similar to a Gibson Les Paul Jr.) outfitted with a humbucker in the bridge and a Floyd Rose whammy system. "Snake" used a Les Paul Jr., also with a Floyd Rose setup. According to producer Michael Wagener, the guitars were all played through an ADA MP-1 preamp, into a McIntosh transistor power amp (2100), through a Marshall 4x12 cab loaded with 30-watt Celestions. The signal was bussed into an EQ and a BBE 802 Sonic Maximizer—a key element to '80s metal guitar tone. (By the way, this was the exact same setup for Extreme's *Pornograffitti* and White Lion's *Pride* albums!)

Given the hair metal sound, pick squeals, and whammy dives, you'll want a super-Strat type of guitar with a humbucker in the bridge and a Floyd Rose or other similar tremolo system. Given that ADA preamps are a bit rare and really only for guitarists playing hair metal, a good substitute would be a master-volume Marshall, such as a JCM 800.

TECHNIQUE

The main riff (Rhy. Fig. 1) is a double-stop classic that appears throughout the tune. Take your time nailing the mini-riff in bar 4, as the shift from the laid-back groove of the first three bars to this rapid-fire, 16th-note descent can be a bit tricky at first. When the Verse comes in, the tone changes to a semi-clean one. Don't switch channels or pickups; rather, turn your guitar's volume knob down about half way to achieve the right sound. This is essential, as you'll then use a volume swell in the last two bars of the Verse, leading into the full-throttle Pre-Chorus.

Sabo takes the first four bars of the solo. You might feel more comfortable fretting the A note on the "and" of beat 4 in bar 1 at the 14th fret of the 3rd string. You also might find it easier to forgo the hammer-ons in the first two beats of bar 3 and instead alternate pick the notes. Also note the ubiquitous presence of pinch harmonics throughout the solo. If you haven't polished this technique, now is a good time to start!

"THE ZOO"
Scorpions

Scorpions guitarist Rudolf Schenker wrote the main riff to "The Zoo" while watching a news report about a tornado. Then, when the band did their first U.S. tour, singer Klaus Meine came up with the lyrics, inspired by the "zoo" that was 1979-era 42nd St. in New York City. Finally, guitarist Mathias Jabs added the famous talk box effect, because he says its "creepiness" matched the lyrical content and feel of the tune. Now *that's* German engineering for ya!

TONE

Schenker naturally played his Gibson Flying V, whereas Jabs preferred his 1963 Fender Strat outfitted with a Bill Lawrence L90 pickup and a Floyd Rose. Both guitarists plugged into Marshall JMP 2204 heads through Marshall 4x12 cabs. Of course, the star of this tune is Jabs's talk box effect.

You'll obviously want a humbucker-equipped guitar to play this tune, plugged into a high-gain tube amp (e.g., Marshall, Orange, Engl). If you either have or are willing to invest in a talk box, you're golden. Otherwise, you can sort of cop this part using a wah pedal, a fuzz pedal, and a whammy bar. Use slow rocker motions and set the fuzz fairly high to capture the grittiness of the part.

TECHNIQUE

The Scorpions are kings of the root–5th–octave power chord, and this Intro marks one of their earliest mega-successes with it. But before you start on that, make sure you tune up a quarter step if you're playing along with the original track.

You'll likely "get" the quarter-note triplet feel simply by playing along with the CD. But if not, it's helpful to understand the architecture of this rhythm. In a quarter-note triplet, which takes up two beats, you play every *other* note of a pair of eighth-note triplets: *trip*-uh-*let*, trip-*uh*-let. Also note that this tune has a shuffle feel, which basically means you play the second of a pair of eighth notes slightly later than normal.

Finally, in measure 18 of the Outro you'll find a double-stop bend at the 14th fret. It's actually a sort of signature piece of the solo. To execute this one properly, bar the 2nd and 3rd strings with your ring finger, and *pull* the string pair down, toward the floor. This helps ensure that the 3rd string is bent a whole step while the 2nd achieves just a half-step displacement.

Back in Black

Words and Music by Angus Young, Malcolm Young and Brian Johnson

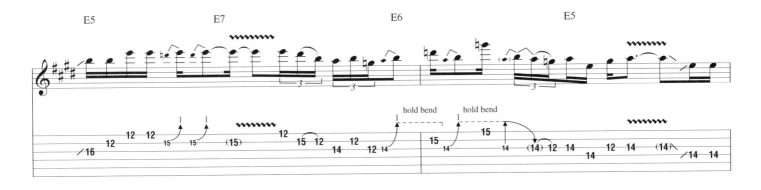

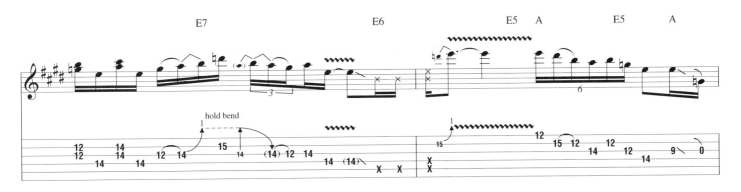

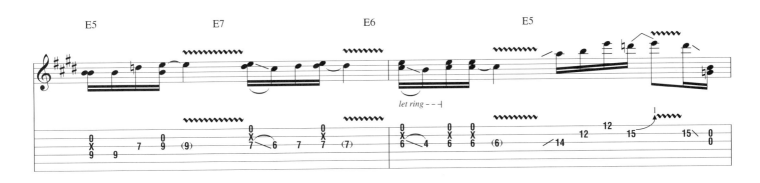

D.S. al Coda

Well, I'm

⊕ Coda

Interlude

w/ Voc. ad lib.

N.C.(E5)

(A5)

(E5)

Well, I'm

Chorus

Gtrs. 1 & 2: w/ Rhy. Fig. 2

A5   E5   B5   A5   B5   A5   E5   B5   A5   B5

back,_____   back._____ Well, I'm
(I'm   back.   I'm

G5   D   A5   G5   A5   G5   D   A5   G5   A5

back,_____   back,_____
back.   I'm   back.   I'm

E5   B5   A5   B5   A5   E5   B5   A5   B5   G5

back,_____   back._____   It's   back   in   black._   Yes, I'm
back.   I'm   back.)

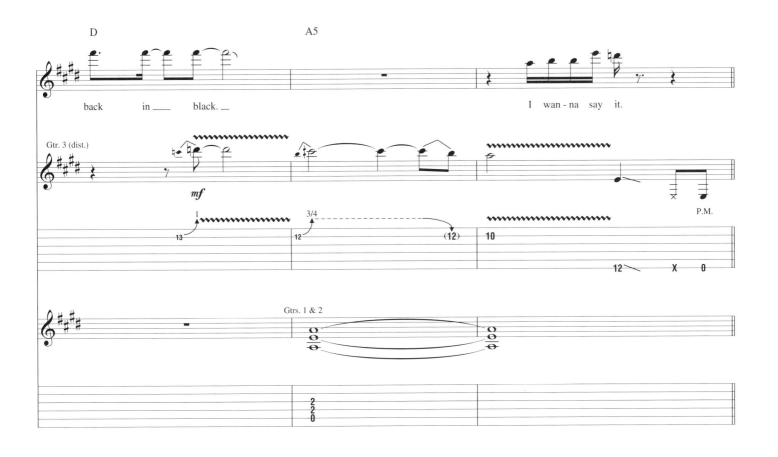

back in ___ black. ___

I wan-na say it.

Outro

Gtrs. 1 & 2: w/ Rhy. Fig. 3 (till fade)

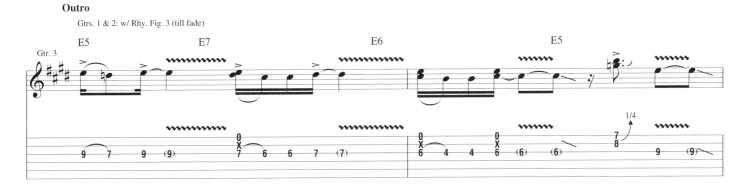

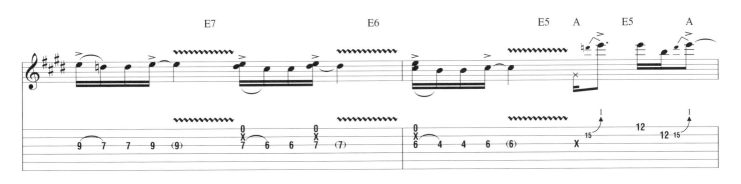

Begin fade

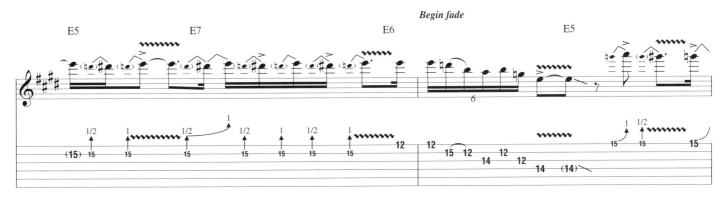

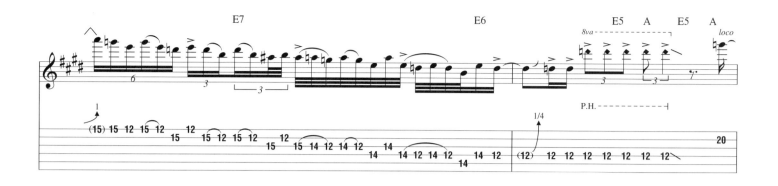

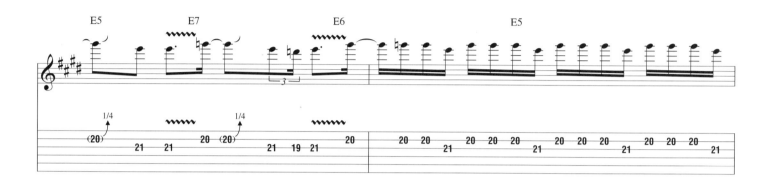

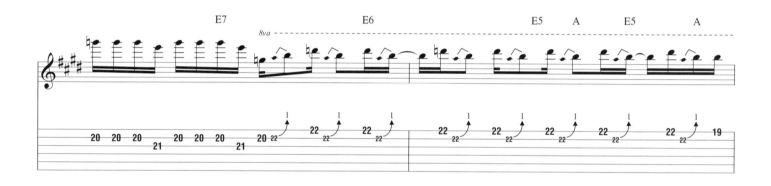

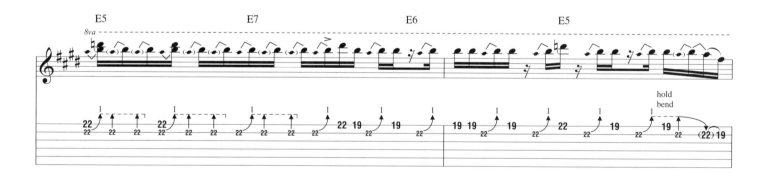

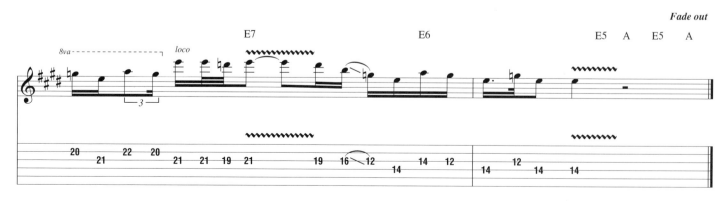

from Van Halen - *5150*

Best of Both Worlds

Words and Music by Edward Van Halen, Alex Van Halen, Michael Anthony and Sammy Hagar

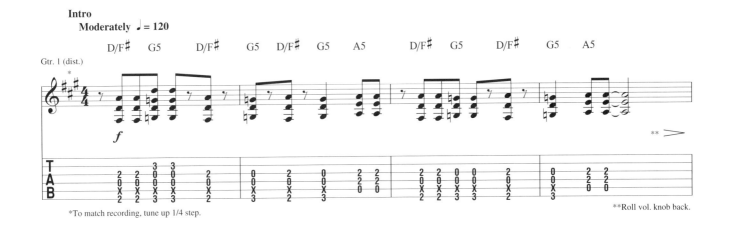

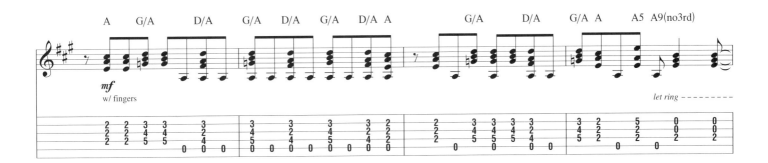

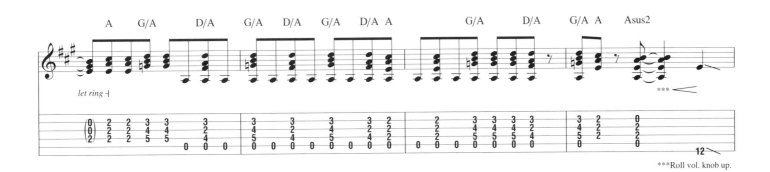

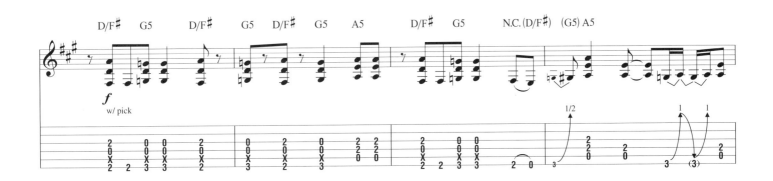

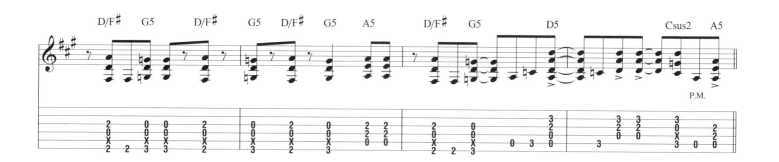

Verse

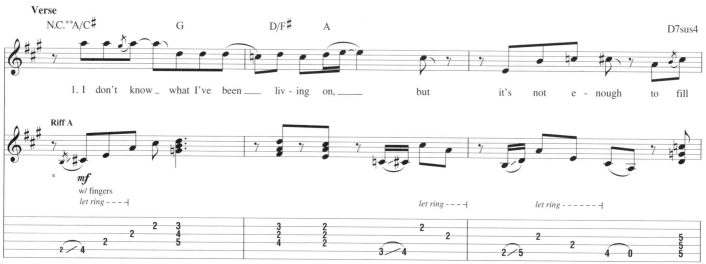

1. I don't know _ what I've been _ liv-ing on, _ but it's not e - nough to fill

*Roll volume knob back.
**Bass plays A throughout verses.

me up. I need more _ than just, a, words can say; _

I need ev-'ry-thing this life can give _ me. Hey, _ hey, _ yeah!

Pre-Chorus

'cause some - thing
Some - thing

reached ____ out and touched ___ me.

Gtr. 1

w/ pick

Gtr. 2 (slight dist.)

mf

let ring - - - - - - - - - - - - - - - -   *let ring* - - - - - - - - - - - - - - - - - -

Now I know   that all I want,   I want the

Gtr. 1

Gtr. 2

let ring - - - - - - - - - - - - - - -

Gtr. 3 (dist.)

f

P.S.

Chorus

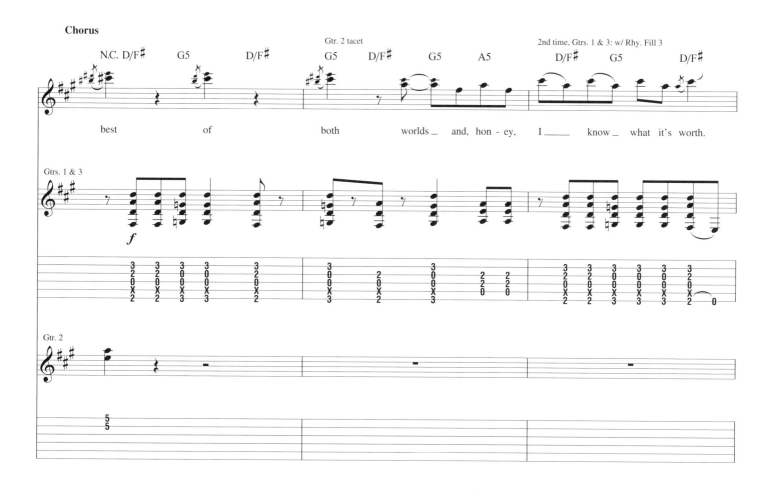

best of both worlds ___ and, hon - ey, I ___ know ___ what it's worth.

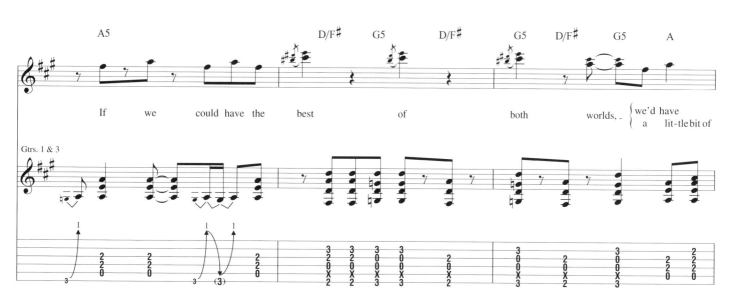

If we could have the best of both worlds, ___ { we'd have / a lit-tle bit of

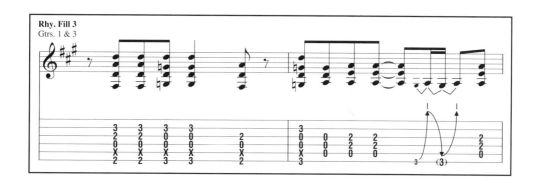

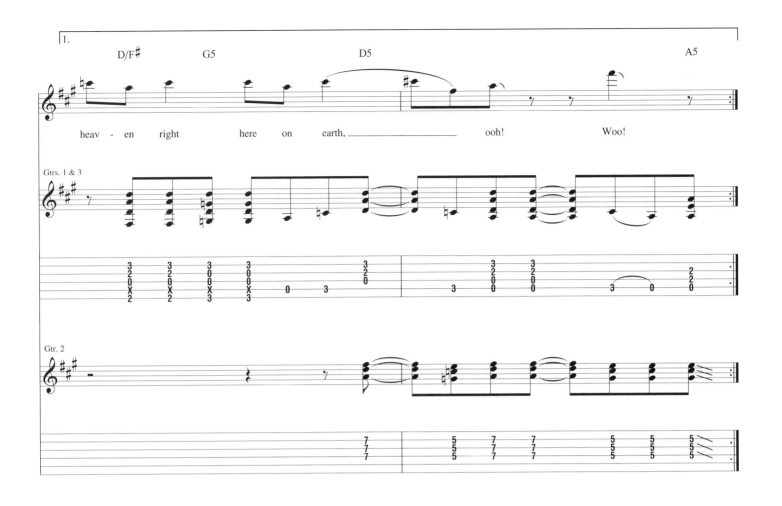

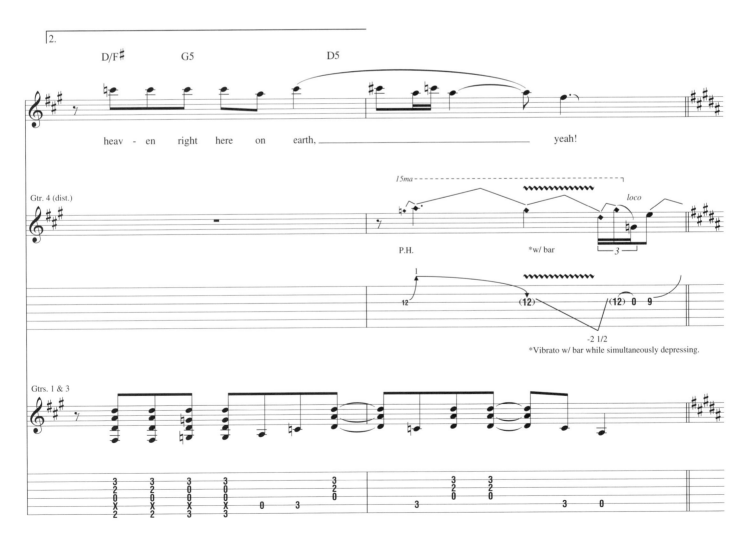

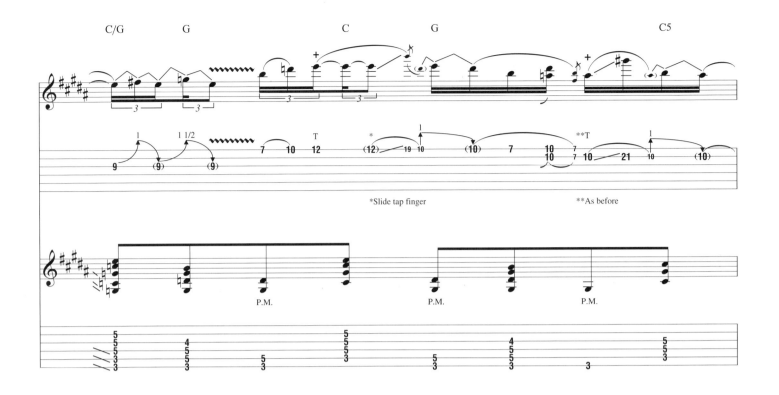

*Slide tap finger   **As before

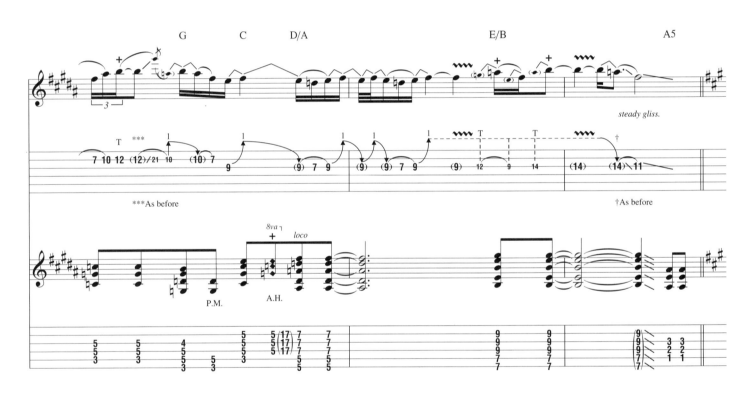

***As before   †As before

Interlude

Gtrs. 3 & 4 tacet

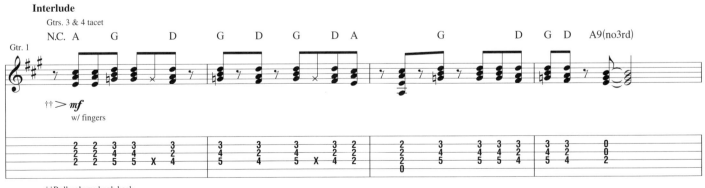

††Roll volume knob back.

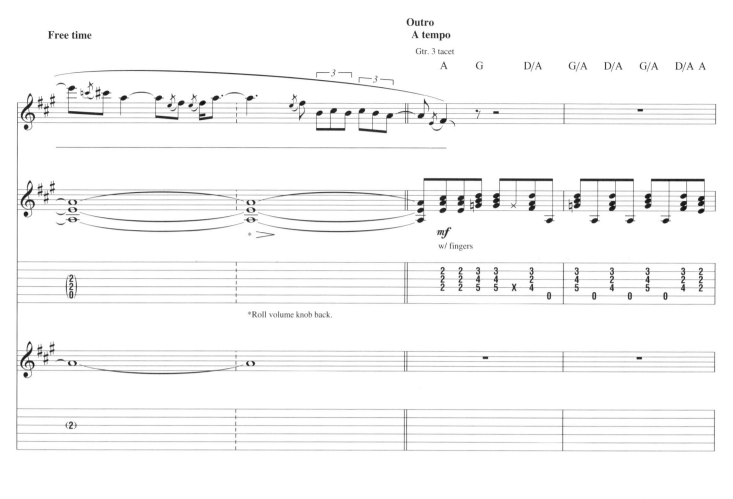

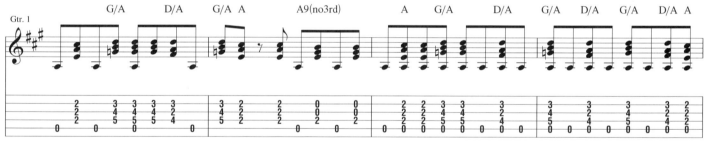

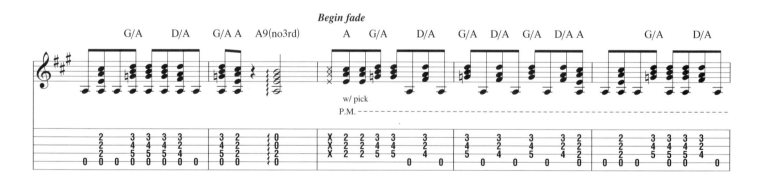

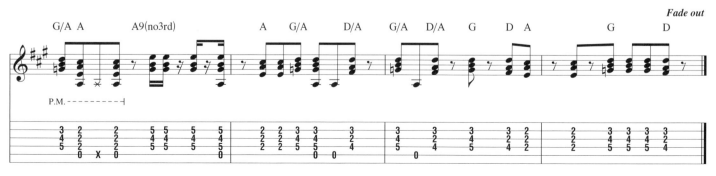

from Ozzy Osbourne - *Blizzard of Ozz*

Crazy Train

Words and Music by Ozzy Osbourne, Randy Rhoads and Bob Daisley

Guitar Solo

from Kiss - *Destroyer*

Detroit Rock City

Words and Music by Paul Stanley and Bob Ezrin

Tune down 1/2 step:
(low to high) E♭-A♭-D♭-G♭-B♭-E♭

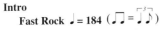

*Chord symbols reflect implied harmony.

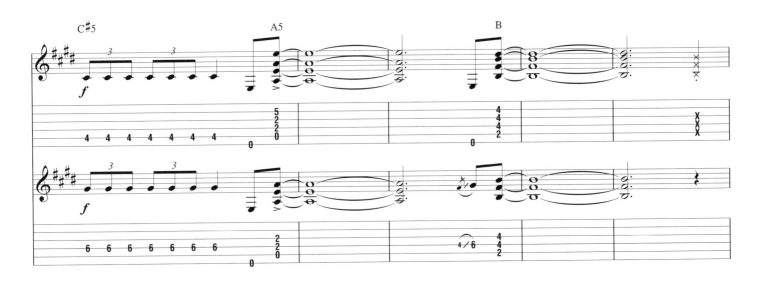

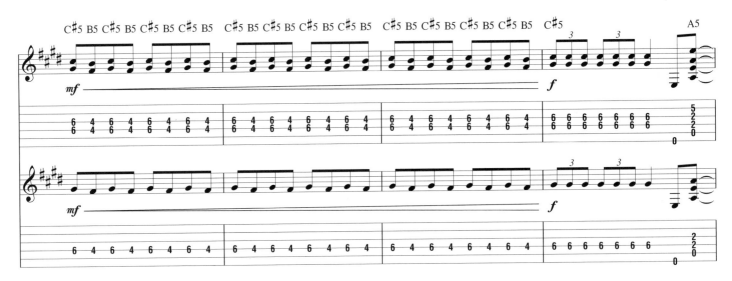

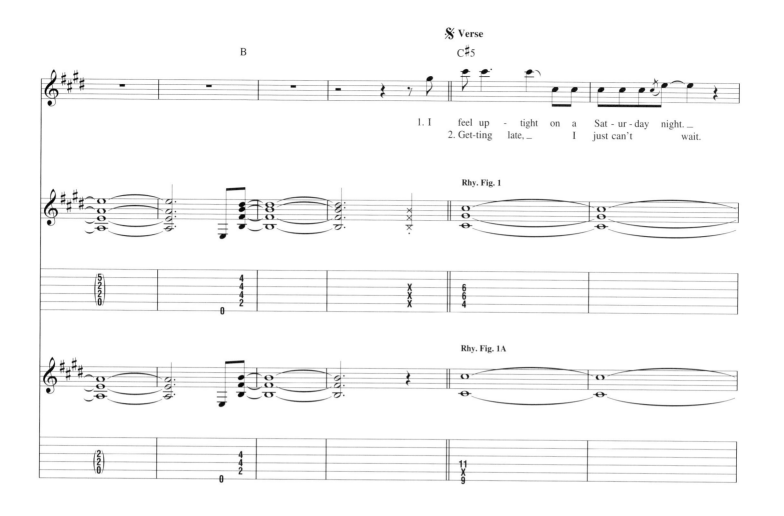

1. I feel up - tight on a Sat - ur - day night.
2. Get - ting late, _ I just can't wait.

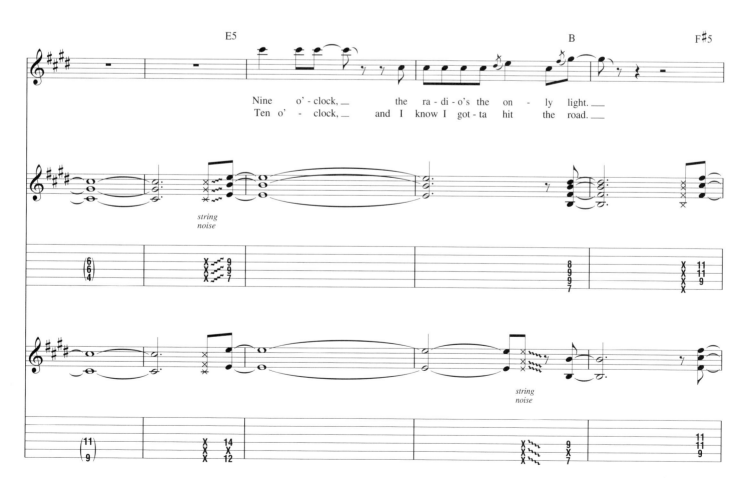

Nine o' - clock, _ the ra - di - o's the on - ly light. _
Ten o' - clock, _ and I know I got - ta hit the road. _

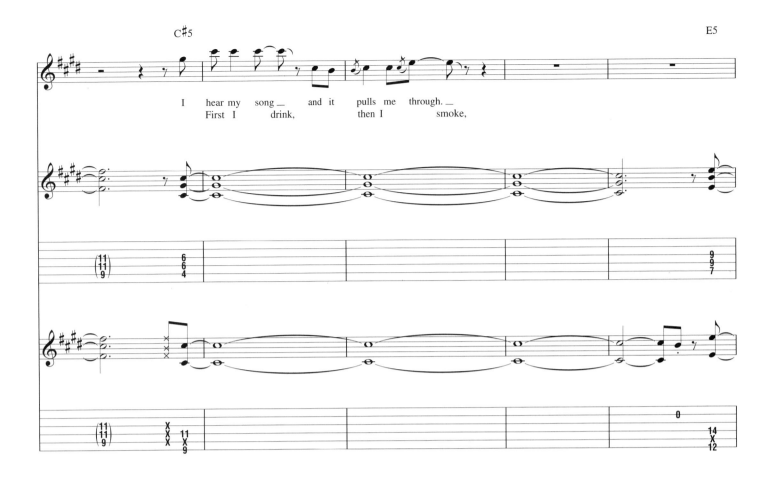

I hear my song___ and it pulls me through.___
First I drink, then I smoke,

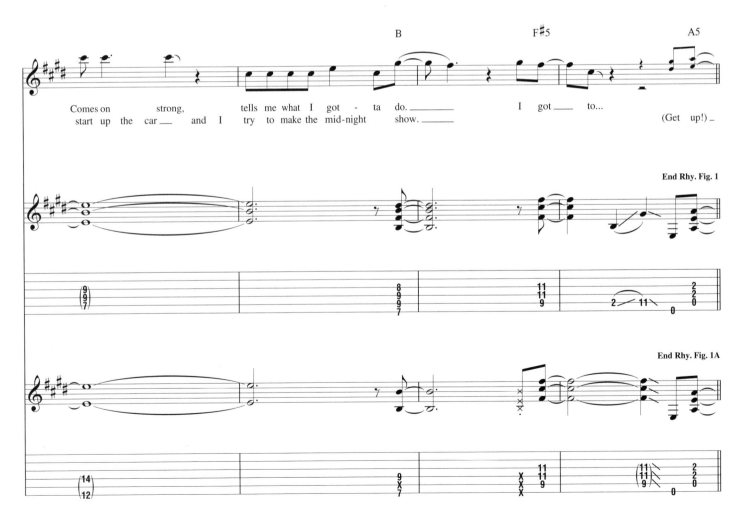

Comes on strong, tells me what I got-ta do.___ I got___ to...
start up the car___ and I try to make the mid-night show.___ (Get up!)___

End Rhy. Fig. 1

End Rhy. Fig. 1A

Chorus

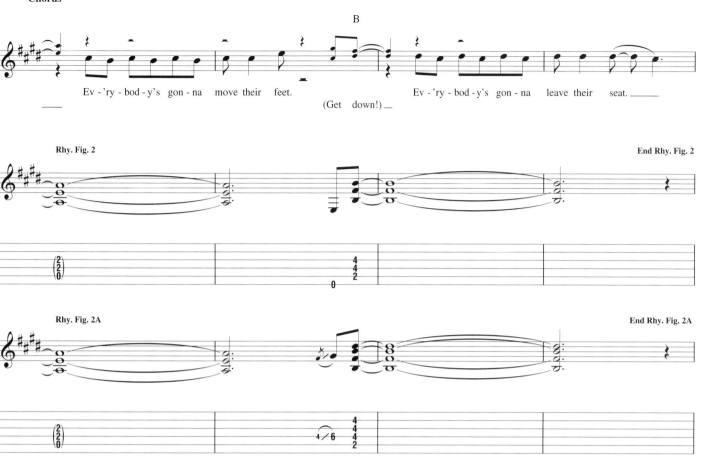

Ev - 'ry - bod - y's gon - na move their feet.   Ev - 'ry - bod - y's gon - na leave their seat. _____

(Get down!) _____

You got - ta lose your mind in De - troit Rock Cit - y.

(Get up!) _____

Verse

Gtr. 1: w/ Rhy. Fig. 1

3. Mov - in' fast, __ do - in' nine - ty - five. __

Gtr. 2

Riff B

fdbk.

Hit top speed, __ but I'm still mov - in' much too slow. _____ I

feel so good, I'm so a - live. __ Hear my song __

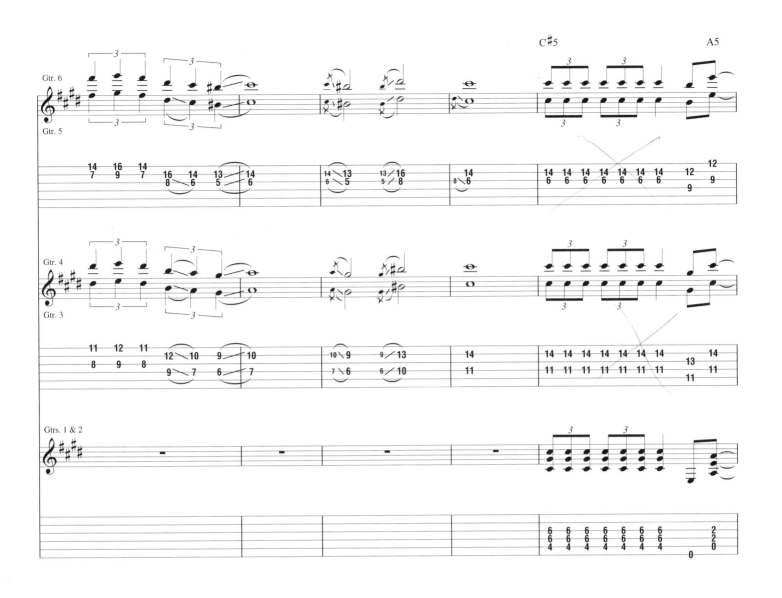

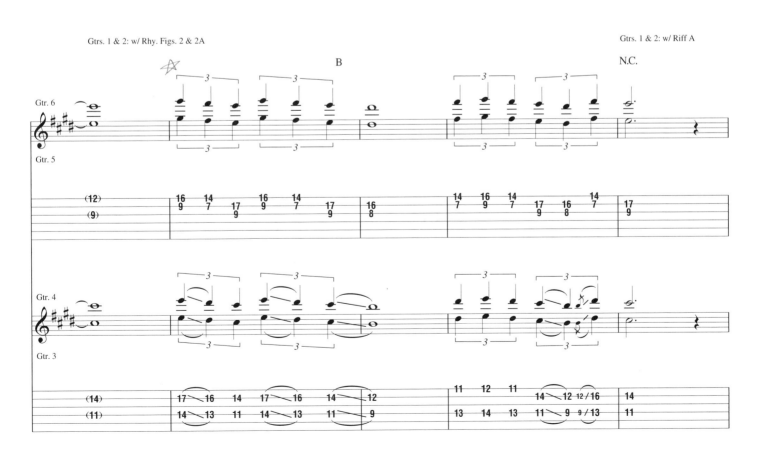

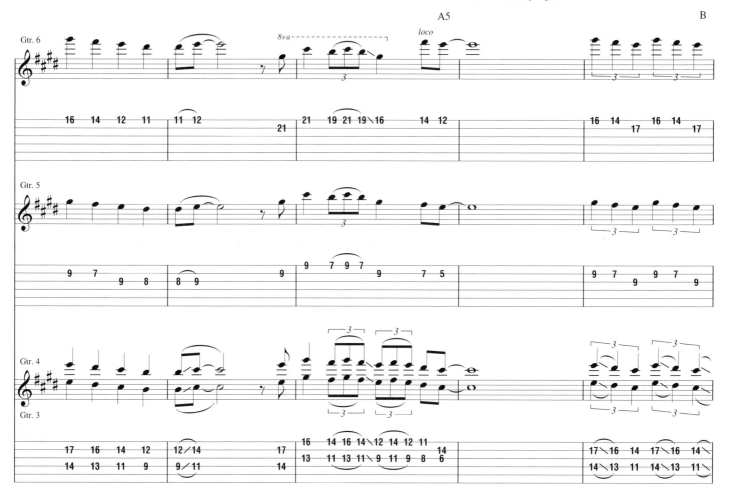

Verse

Gtr. 1: w/ Rhy. Fig 1
Gtr. 2: w/ Riff B
Gtrs. 5 & 6 tacet

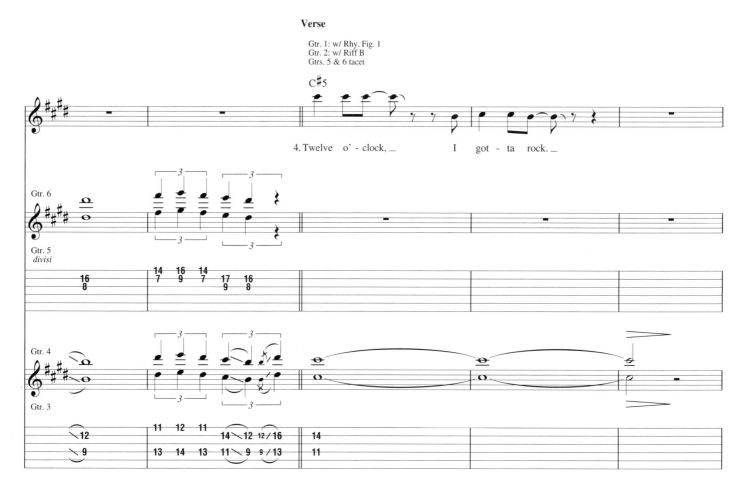

4. Twelve o' - clock, ___ I got - ta rock. ___

Gtrs. 3 & 4 tacet

There's a truck a - head, __ lights star - in' at my eyes. _____

Oh, my God, _ no time to turn. _

I

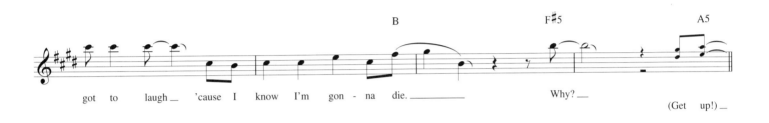

got to laugh _ 'cause I know I'm gon - na die. _____ Why? _ (Get up!) _

Outro-Chorus

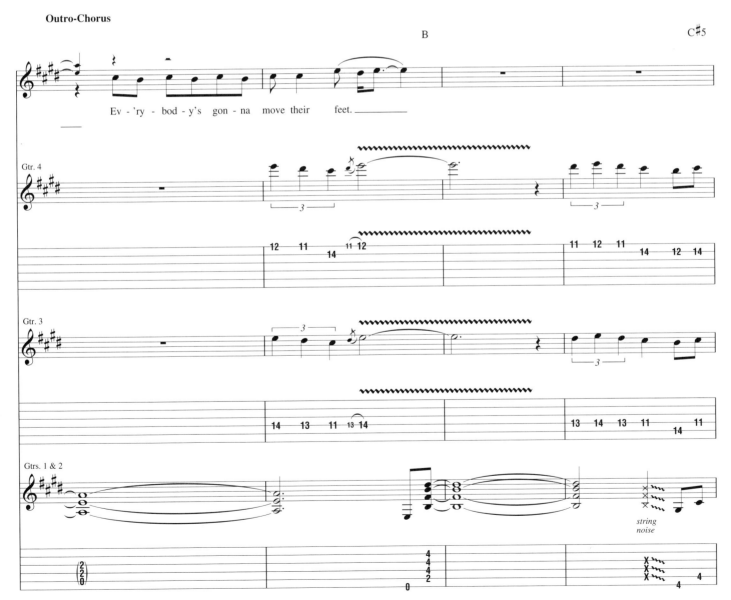

Ev - 'ry - bod - y's gon - na move their feet. _____

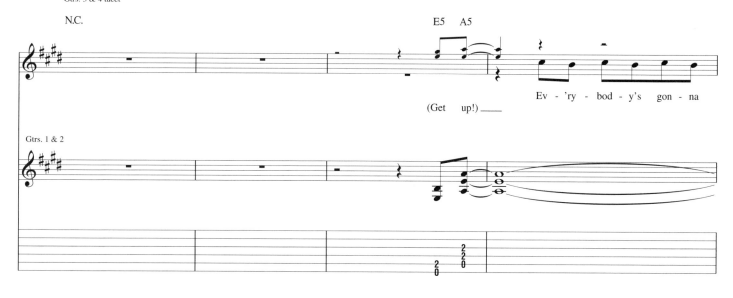

from UFO - *Phenomenon*

Doctor, Doctor

Words and Music by Phillip John Mogg and Michael Schenker

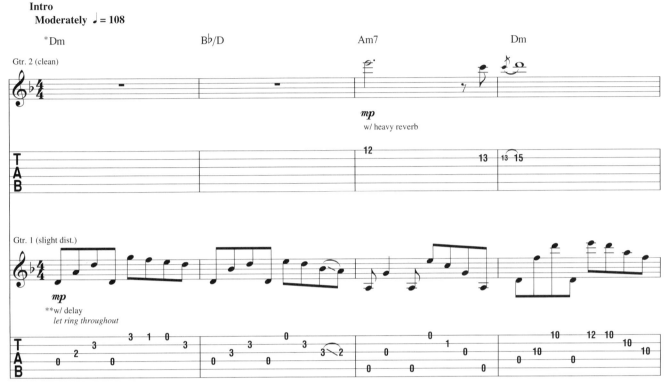

*Chord symbols reflect implied harmony.

**Set for sixteenth-note regeneration w/ 1 repeat.

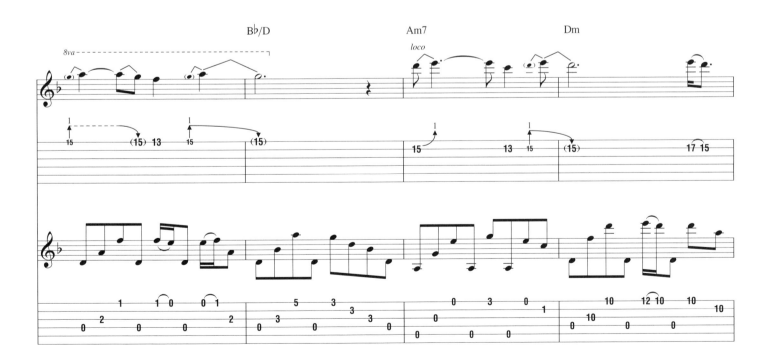

Chorus

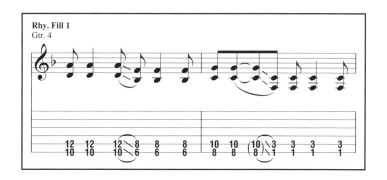

Rhy. Fill 1
Gtr. 4

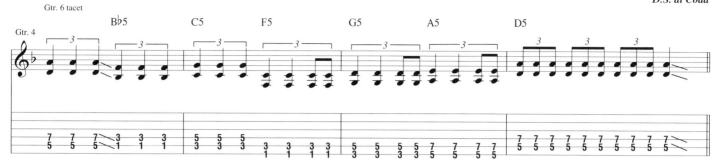

✦ Coda

Interlude

Gtrs. 3 & 5: w/ Riffs A & A1
Gtr. 4: w/ Rhy. Fig. 1

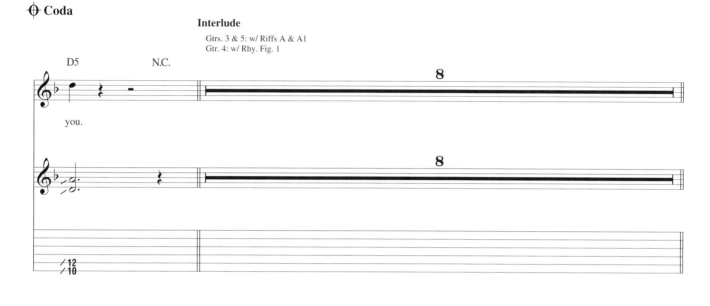

you.

Outro

Gtrs. 3 & 5: w/ Riffs A & A1 (till fade)
Gtr. 4: w/ Rhy. Fig. 1 (till fade)

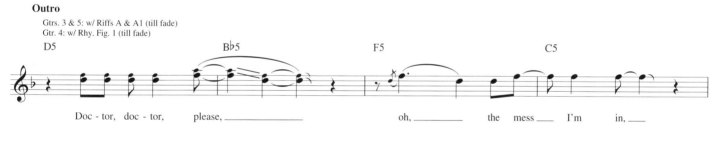

Doc - tor, doc - tor, please, _____ oh, _____ the mess _____ I'm in, _____

Begin fade

doc - tor, doc - tor, please, _____ oh, I'm go - in' fast. ___

Doc - tor, doc - tor, please, _____ oh, _____ the mess I'm in, _____

Fade out

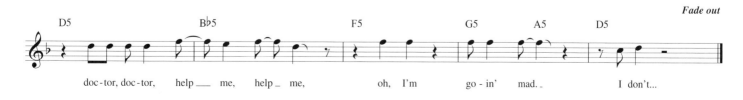

doc - tor, doc - tor, help ___ me, help _ me, oh, I'm go - in' mad. _ I don't...

Fire Woman

Words and Music by Ian Astbury and William Duffy

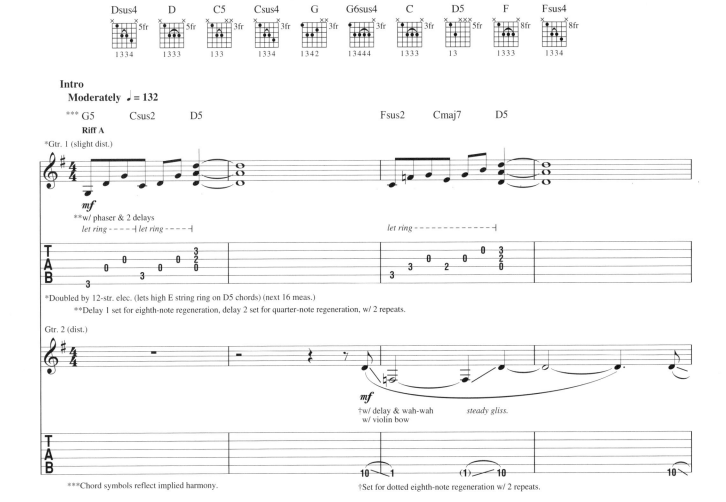

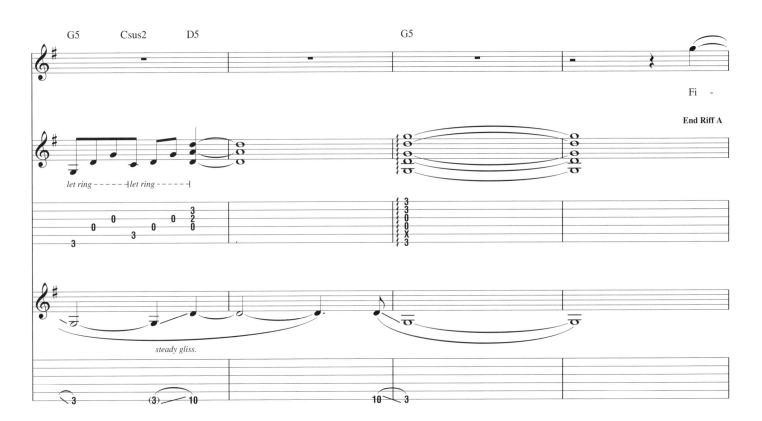

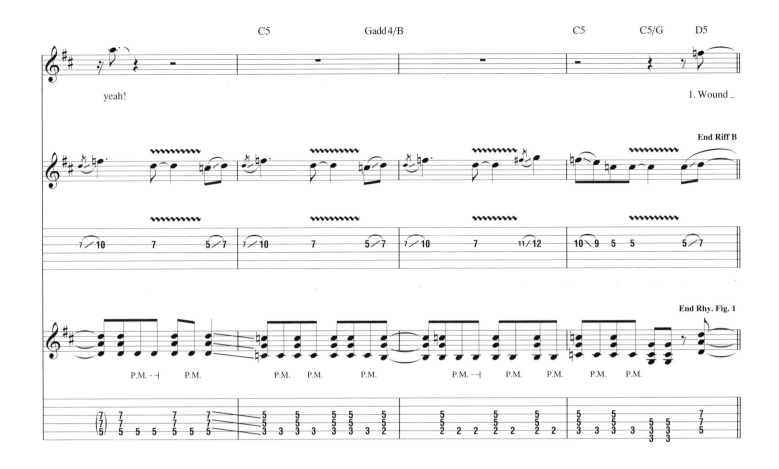

yeah!

1. Wound _

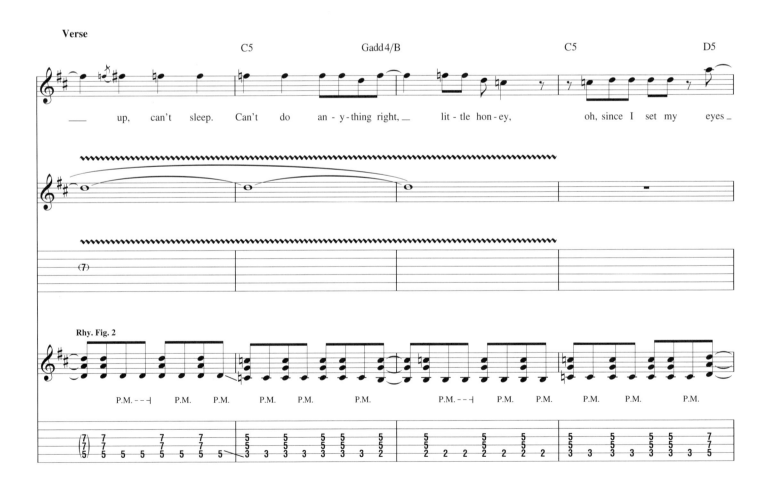

Verse

_ up, can't sleep. Can't do an-y-thing right, _ lit-tle hon-ey, oh, since I set my eyes _

*w/ phaser. Doubled by 12-str. elec. (next 15 meas.).

from Nazareth - *Hair of the Dog*

Hair of the Dog

Words and Music by Dan McCafferty, Darrell Sweet, Pete Agnew and Manuel Charlton

Red hot ma-ma, vel-vet charm-er, time's come to pay your dues. __

Gtr. 1

Gtr. 2

Gtr. 1: w/ Riff A

Gtr. 2

P.M.

§ Chorus

E5 N.C.   G5   A5 N.C.   E5 N.C.   D5   E5   N.C.

Now you're mess-in' with a...   Now you're mess-in' with a   son of a bitch. _

Voc. Fig. 1   End Voc. Fig. 1

(A son of a bitch.) _____

Rhy. Fig. 1   End Rhy. Fig. 1

Gtr. 1

Gtr. 2

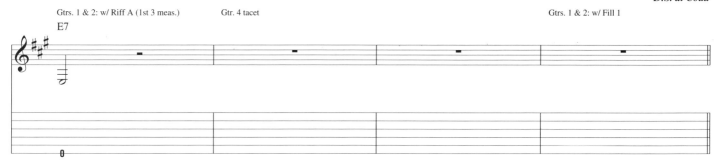

Coda

Outro

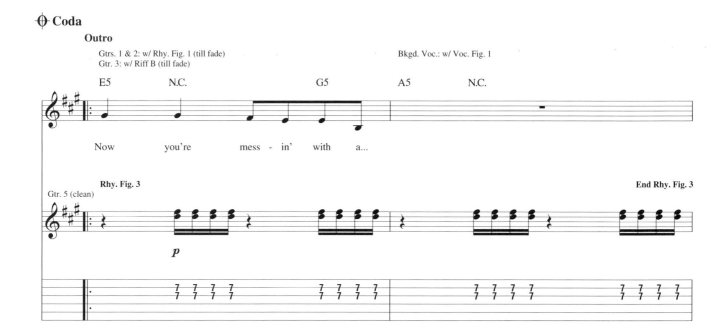

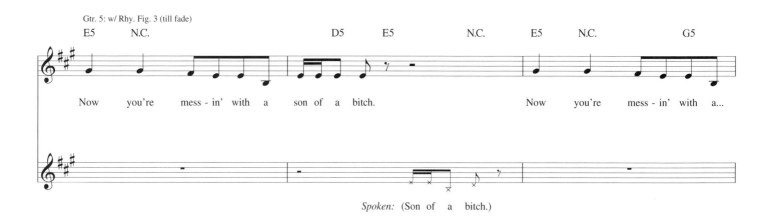

Spoken: (Son of a bitch.)

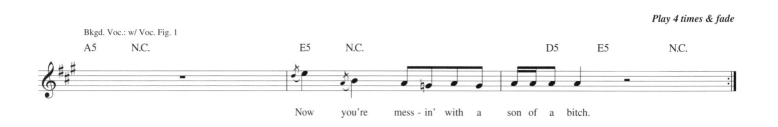

from Dokken - *Under Lock and Key*

In My Dreams

Words and Music by Don Dokken, George Lynch, Jeff Pilson and Mick Brown

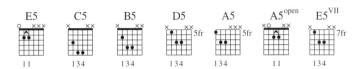

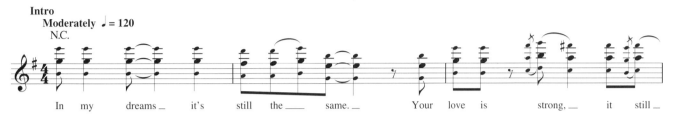

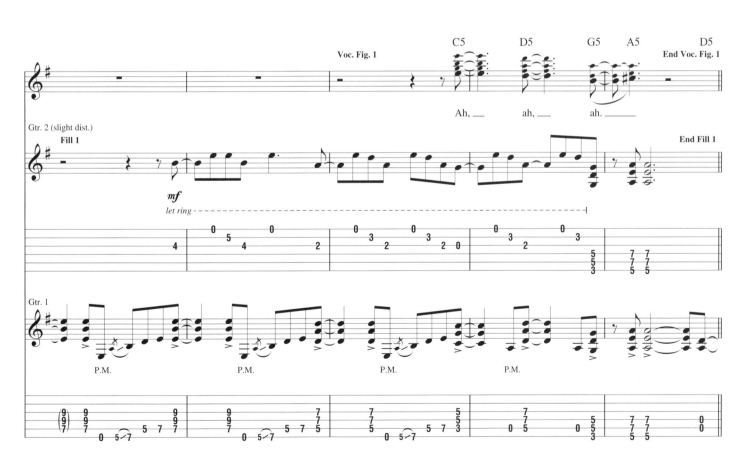

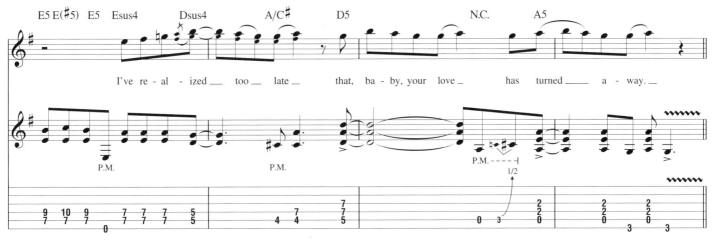

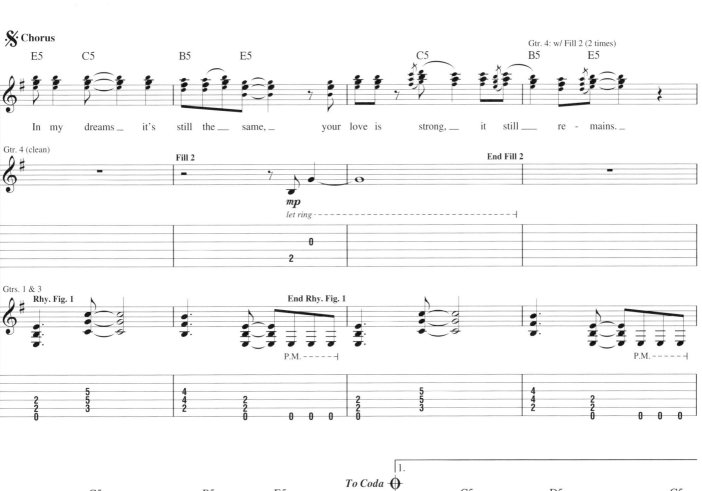

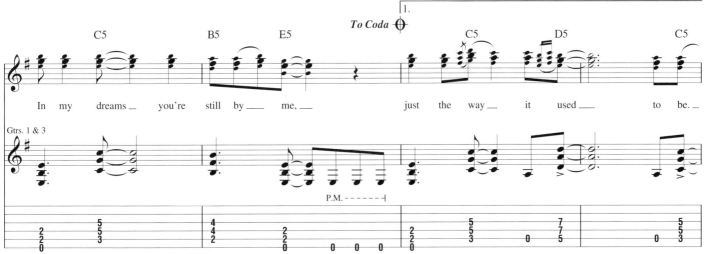

just the way ___ it used ___ to be. ___

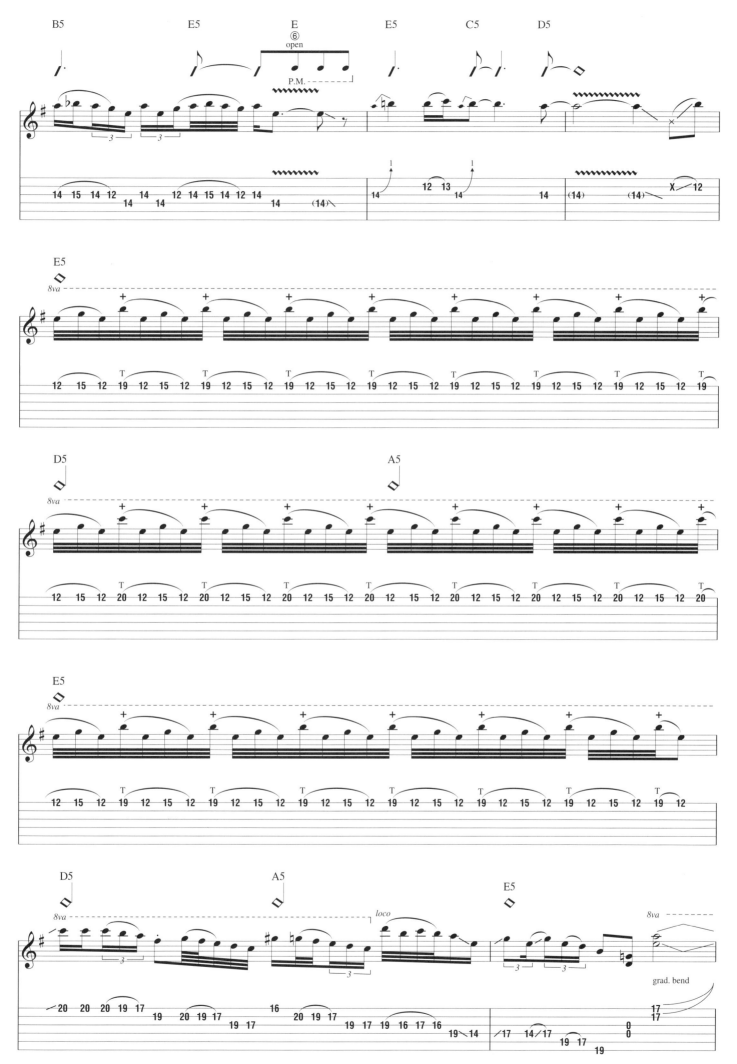

from Iron Butterfly - *In-a-Gadda-da-Vida*

In-a-Gadda-da-Vida
Words and Music by Doug Ingle

*Chord symbols reflect overall harmony.

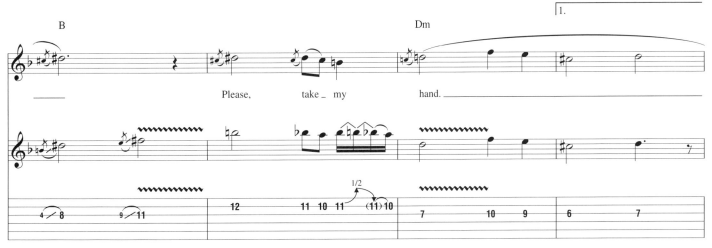

Gtr. 1: w/ Riff A

Let me take your hand.

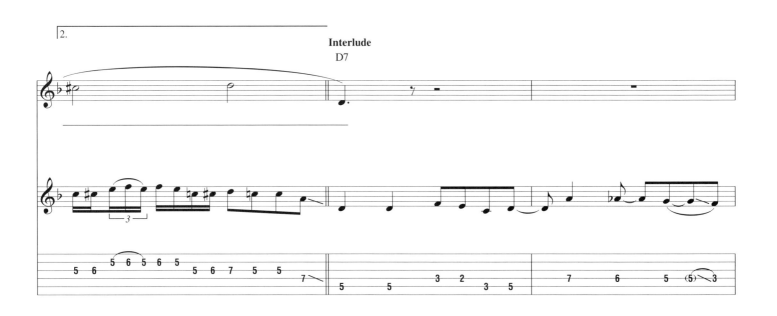

Interlude

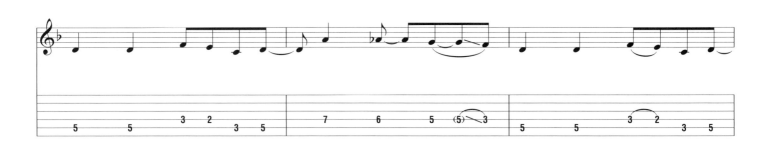

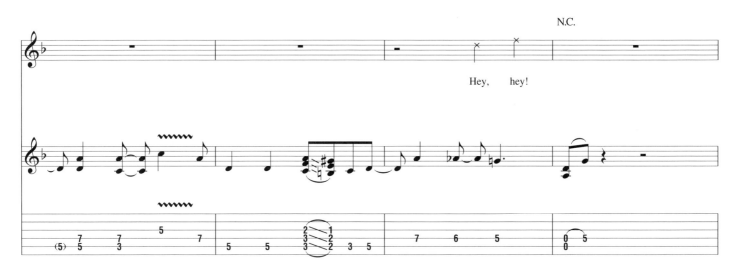

N.C.

Hey,   hey!

All right now, ah!

Outro

D7

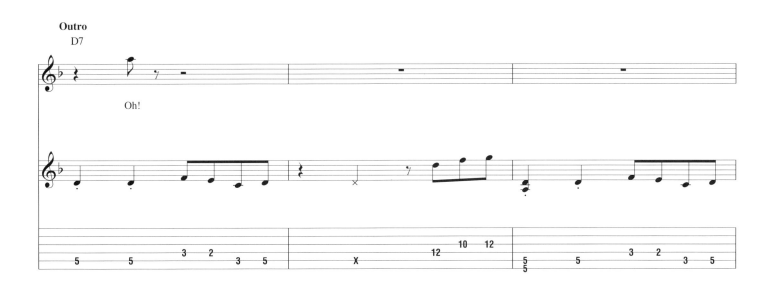

Oh!

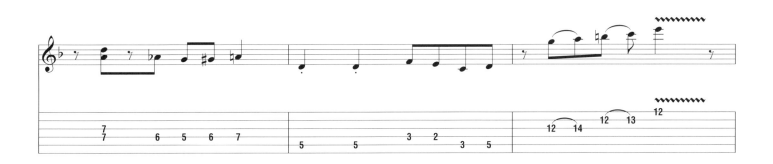

N.C.

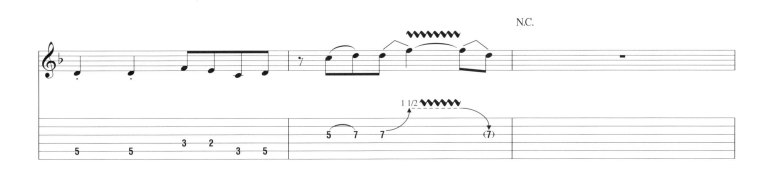

D7

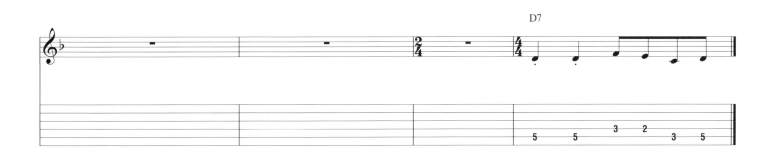

from **Thin Lizzy** - *Jailbreak*

Jailbreak

Words and Music by Philip Parris Lynott

**Composite arrangement

from Cinderella - *Night Songs*

Nobody's Fool

Words and Music by Tom Keifer

Intro
Slow Rock ♩ = 68

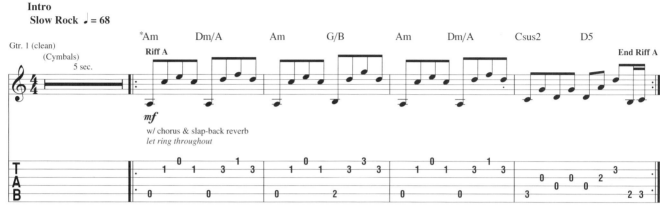

*Chord symbols reflect implied harmony.

𝄋 Verse

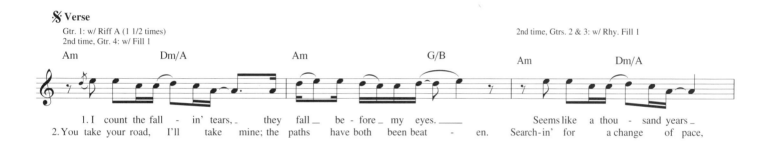

1. I count the fall - in' tears, _ they fall be - fore _ my eyes. _____ Seems like a thou - sand years _
2. You take your road, I'll take mine; the paths have both been beat - en. Search-in' for a change of pace,

since we broke the ties. _ I call you on _ the phone, _ but nev - er get a rise. _
life needs to be sweet - ened. I scream ___ my heart _ out just to make a dime, _ and

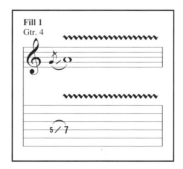

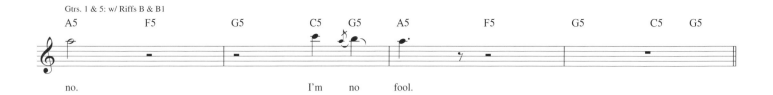

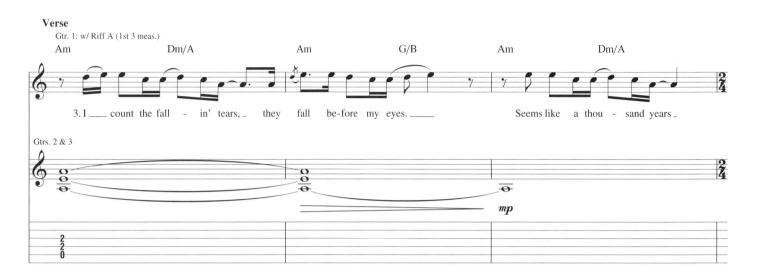

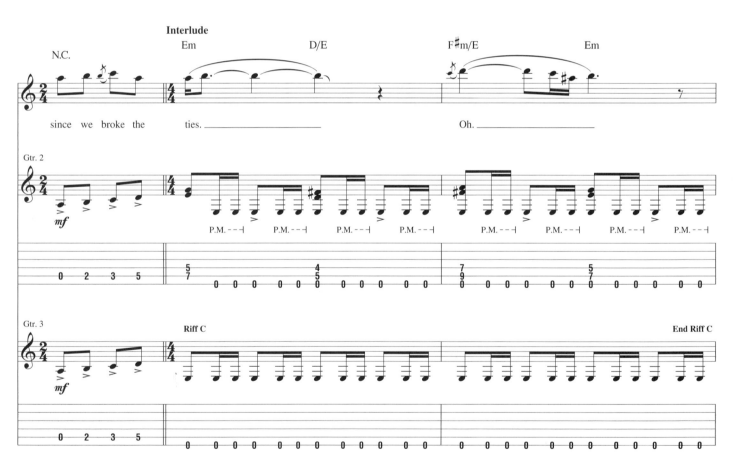

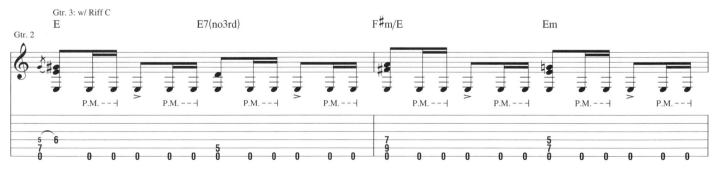

98

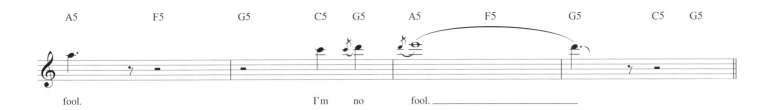

fool.   I'm no   fool. _____

Outro-Guitar Solo

Bkgd. Voc.: w/ Voc. Fig. 1 (2 times)
Gtrs. 1 & 5: w/ Riffs B & B1 (till fade)
Gtrs. 2 & 3: w/ Rhy. Fig. 1 (till fade)

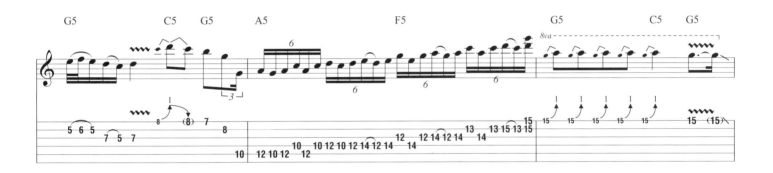

Begin fade

Bkgd. Voc.: w/ Voc. Fig. 1 (till fade)

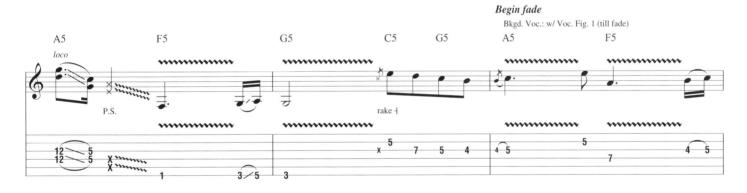

Fade out

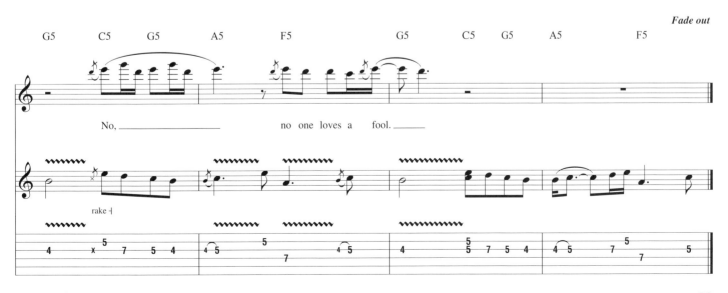

No, _____   no one loves a   fool. _____

from Black Sabbath - *Paranoid*

Paranoid

Words and Music by Anthony Iommi, John Osbourne, William Ward and Terence Butler

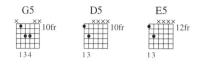

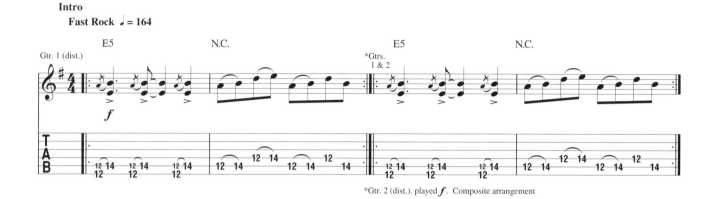

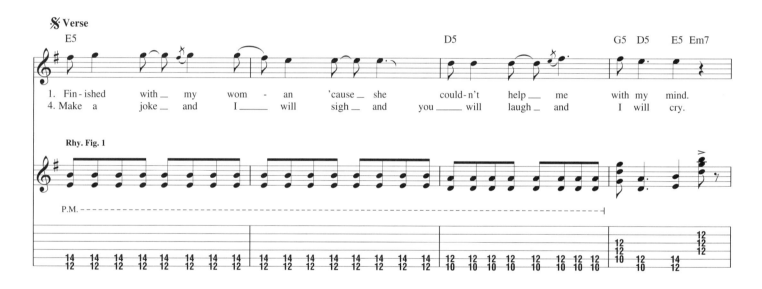

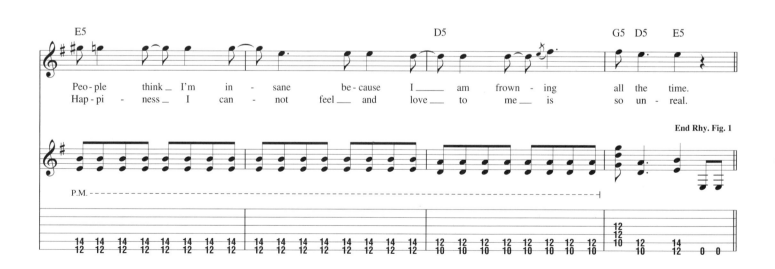

Interlude

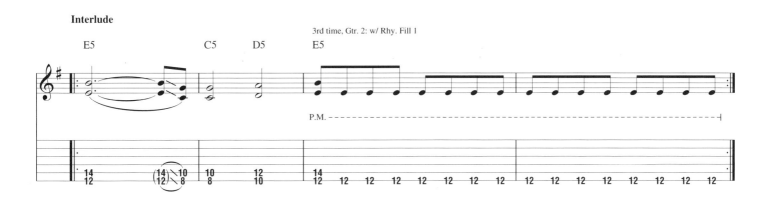

Verse

1st time, Gtrs. 1 & 2: w/ Rhy. Fig. 1
2nd time, Gtrs. 1 & 2: w/ Rhy. Fig. 1 (1st 4 meas., 2 times)

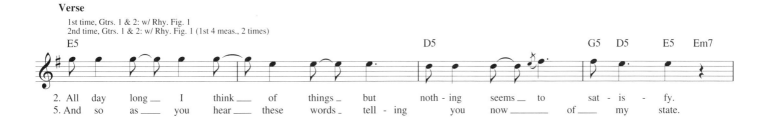

2. All day long ___ I think ___ of things ___ but ___ noth - ing seems ___ to sat - is - fy.
5. And so as ___ you hear ___ these words ___ tell - ing you now ___ of ___ my state.

To Coda ⊕

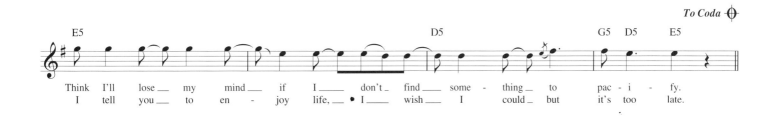

Think I'll lose ___ my mind ___ if I ___ don't ___ find ___ some - thing ___ to pac - i - fy.
I tell you ___ to en - joy life, ___ • I ___ wish ___ I could ___ but it's too late.

Bridge

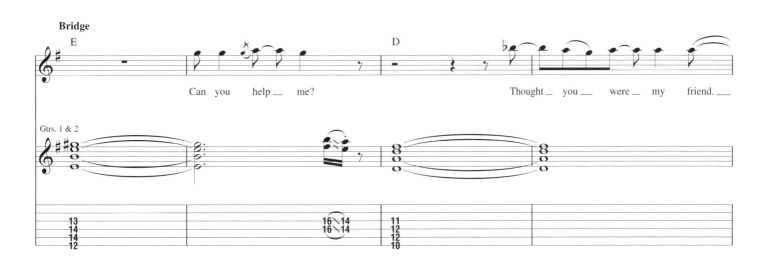

Can you help ___ me?   Thought ___ you ___ were ___ my friend.

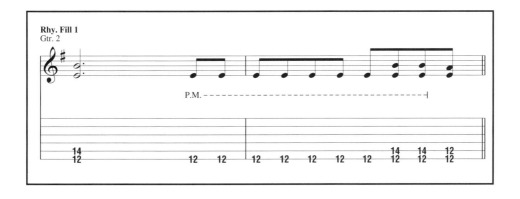

Rhy. Fill 1
Gtr. 2

Whoa, _____ yeah! _____

string noise

Interlude

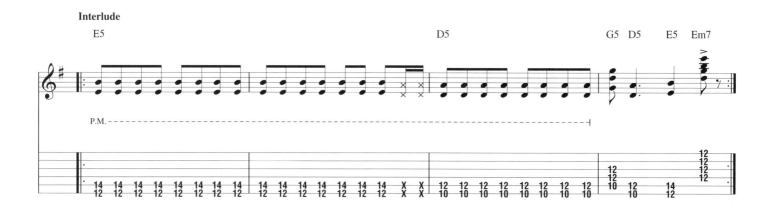

Verse

Gtrs. 1 & 2: w/ Rhy. Fig. 1

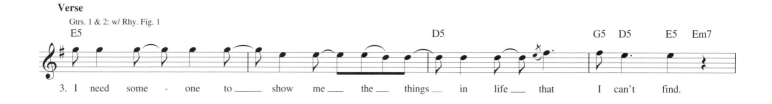

3. I need some - one to ___ show me ___ the ___ things ___ in life ___ that I can't find.

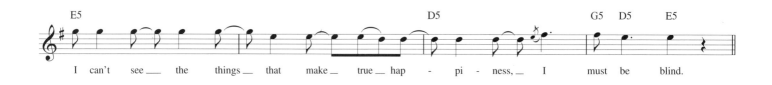

I can't see ___ the things ___ that make ___ true ___ hap - pi - ness, ___ I must be blind.

Guitar Solo

Gtrs. 1 & 2: w/ Rhy. Fig. 1 (1st 4 meas., 4 times)

*Gtr. 3 (dist.)

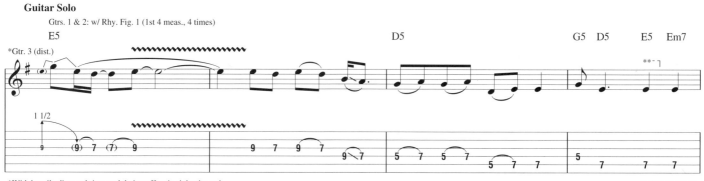

*With heavily distorted ring modulation effect in right channel.

**Played ahead of the beat.

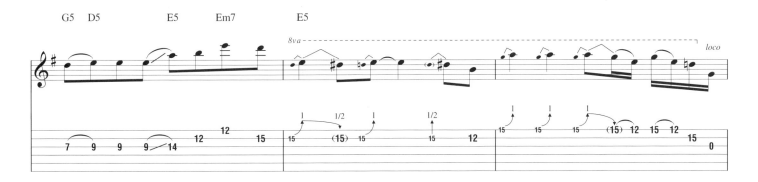

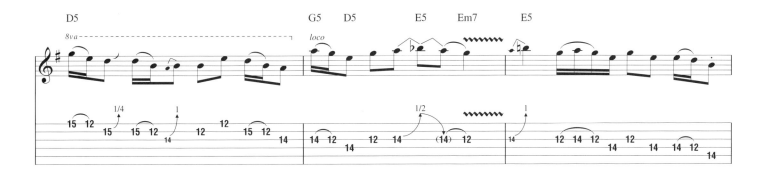

Interlude

D.S. al Coda

Gtrs. 1 & 2: w/ Rhy. Fig. 1 (1st 4 meas., 2 times)
Gtr. 3 tacet

⊕ Coda

Outro

Gtrs. 1 & 2: w/ Rhy. Fig. 1 (1st 7 meas.)

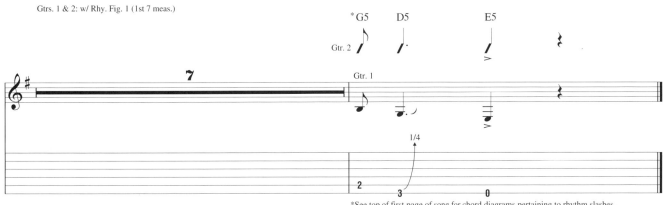

*See top of first page of song for chord diagrams pertaining to rhythm slashes.

from Montrose - *Montrose*

Rock Candy

Words and Music by Sammy Hagar and Ronnie Montrose

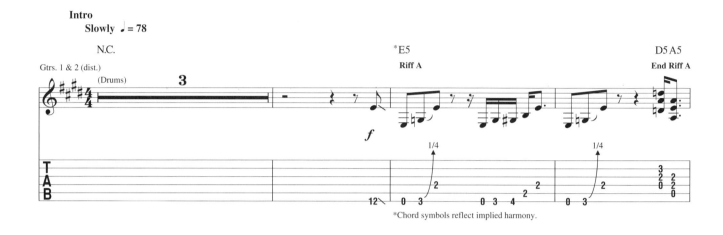

*Chord symbols reflect implied harmony.

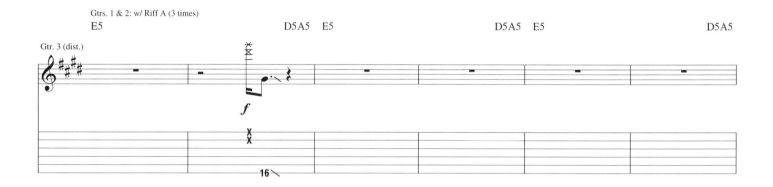

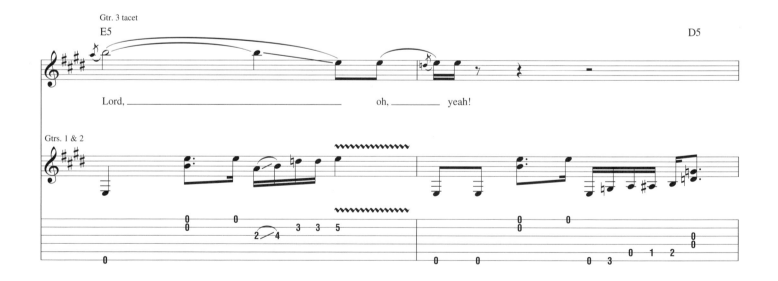

Lord, _____ oh, _____ yeah!

Chorus

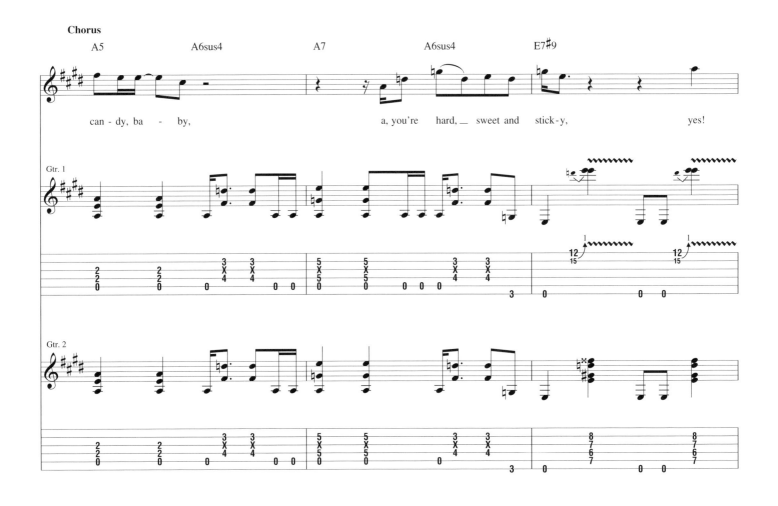

can - dy, ba - by,   a, you're   hard, _ sweet and   stick-y,   yes!

But you're rock   can - dy, ba - by,   hard, _ sweet and

stick-y, _____   yes, _____   oh! _____

Guitar Solo

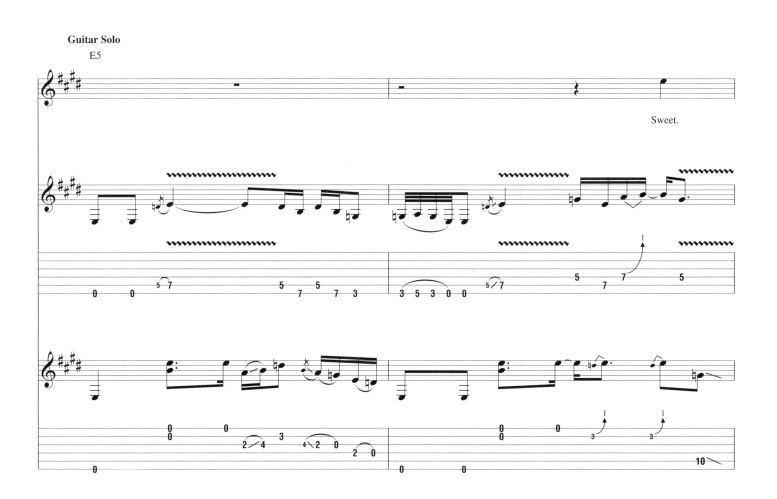

Sweet.

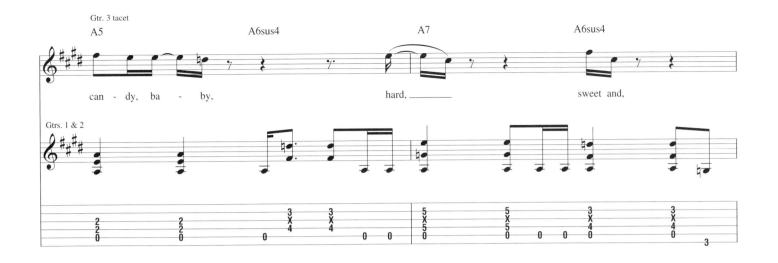

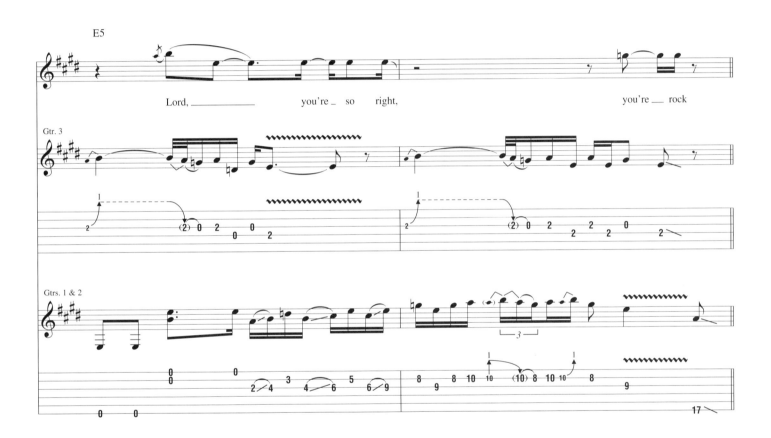

Outro

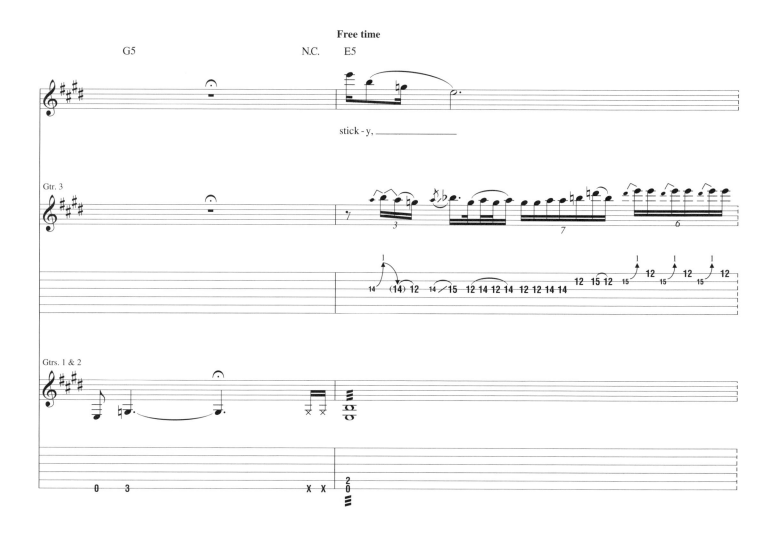

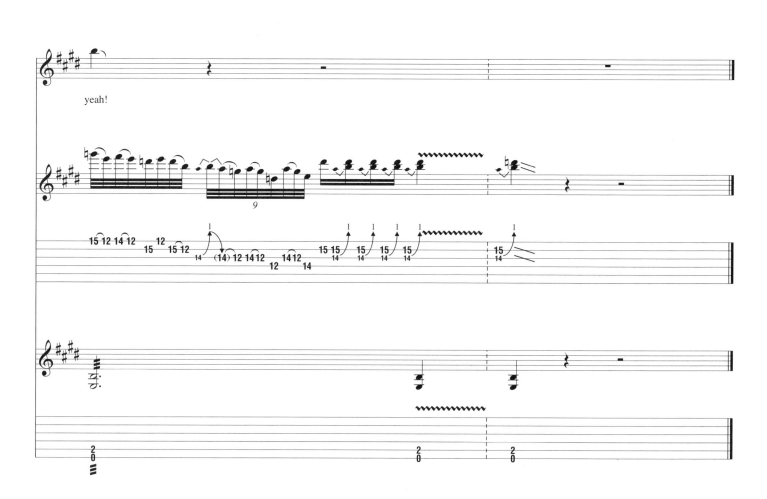

from Def Leppard - *Pyromania*

Rock of Ages

Words and Music by Joe Elliott, Richard Savage, Richard Allen, Steve Clark, Peter Willis and R.J. Lange

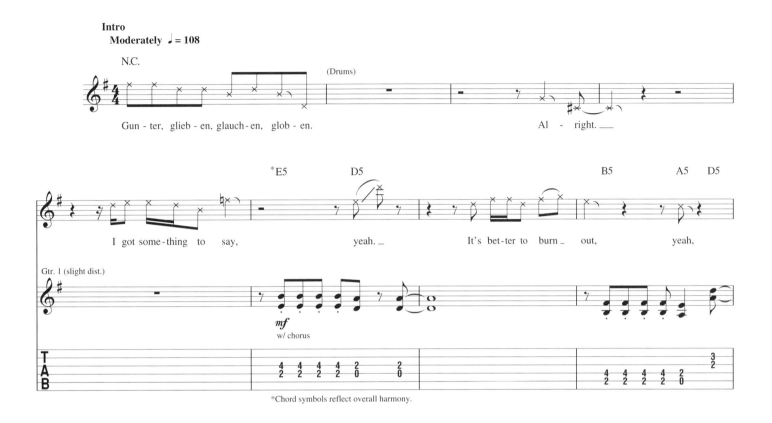

*Chord symbols reflect overall harmony.

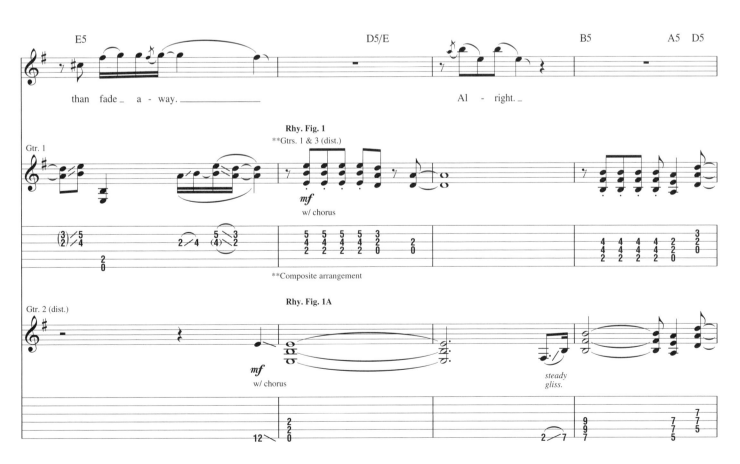

**Composite arrangement

gim - me, gim - me, gim - me, gim - me one more __ for the road, __ yeah.

Pitch: E   F#

Bridge

Gtrs. 1 & 3: w/ Rhy. Fig. 2

A5   G5   N.C.   A5   G5   N.C.   E5   G5   A5

What do you want? __   What __ do __ you want? ____   I ____ want rock 'n' roll. __

Guitar Solo

N.C.   A5   E5   E5   N.C.

You bet ya!   Long __ live __ rock 'n' roll. __   Ah,   yes!

Gtr. 4 (dist.)

mf

P.H.   slight P.H.

grad. bend

Pitch: F#

w/ bar
grad. dive

Harm.

w/ bar

Pitch: G
        D

-1/2   -1   -1 1/2   -2 1/2

School's Out

Words and Music by Alice Cooper and Michael Bruce

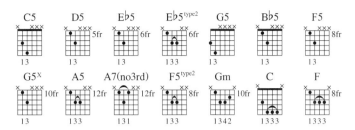

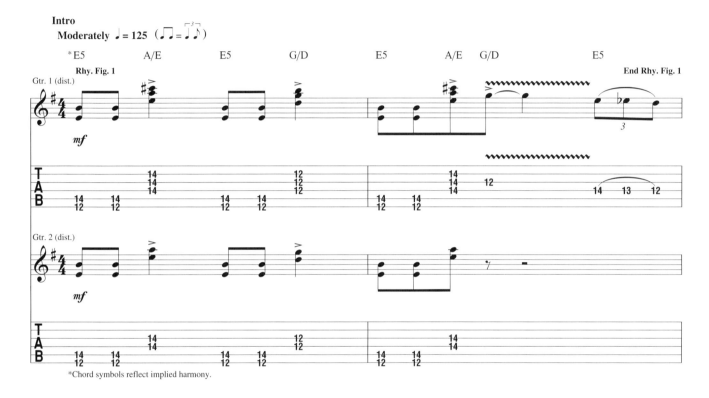

*Chord symbols reflect implied harmony.

**Vol. swell in specified rhythm (studio effect).

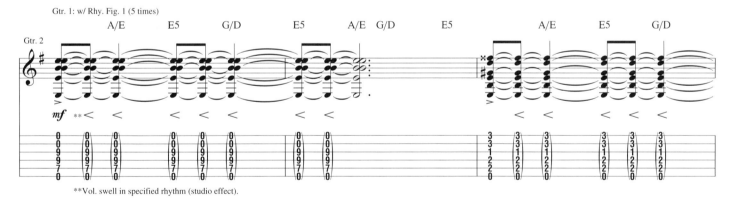

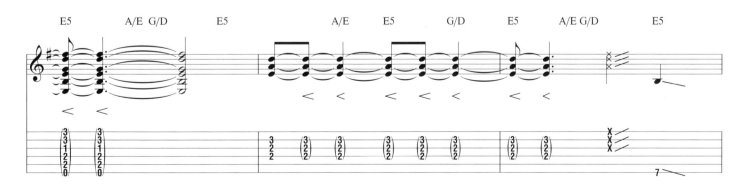

Pre-Chorus

can't sa - lute __ ya, can't find a flag. __ If that don't suit ya, that's a drag. __

*See top of first page of song for chord diagrams pertaining to rhythm slashes.

Chorus

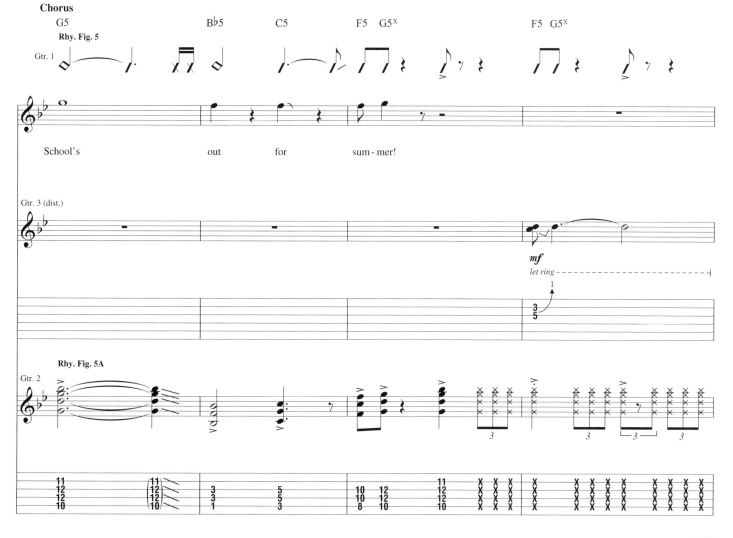

School's out for sum - mer!

School's   out   for   -   ev - er!

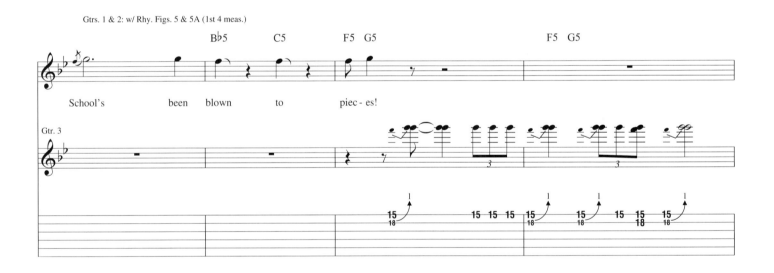

School's   been   blown   to   piec - es!

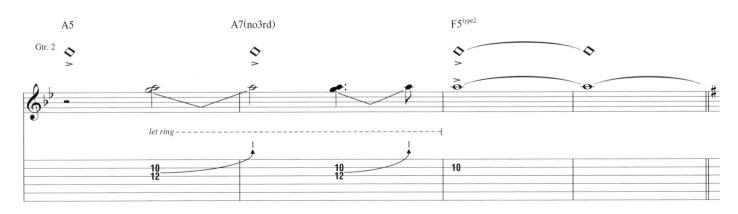

Bridge

Gtr. 2 tacet

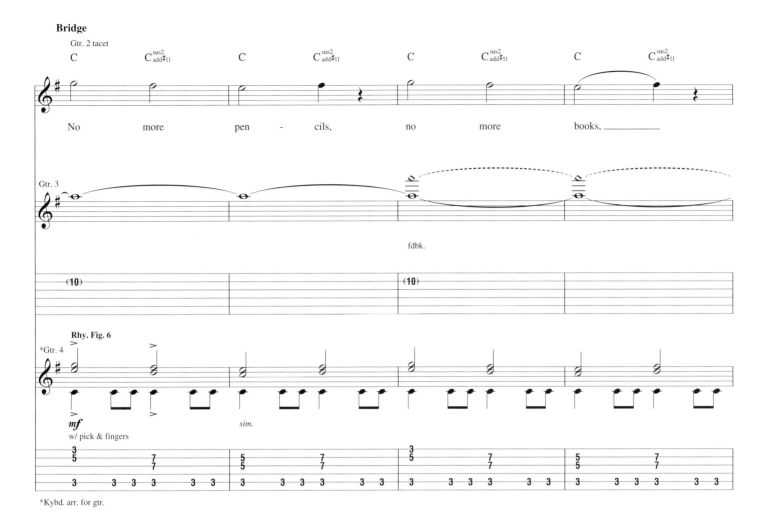

No more pen-cils, no more books,

fdbk.

Rhy. Fig. 6

*Gtr. 4

mf

w/ pick & fingers

sim.

*Kybd. arr. for gtr.

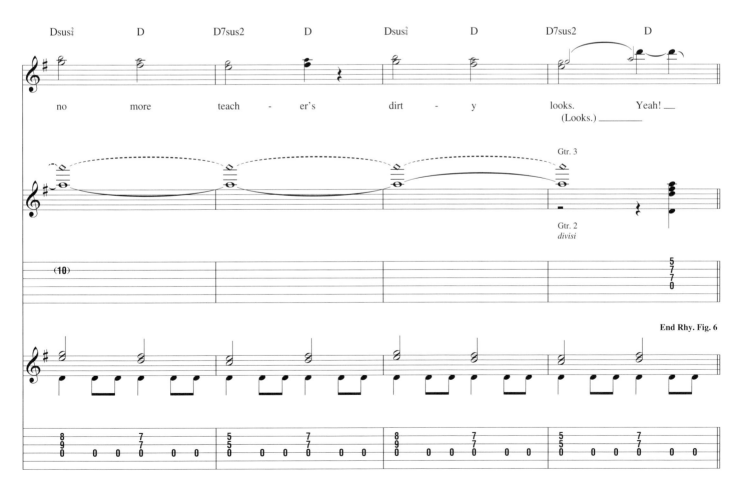

no more teach-er's dirt-y looks. Yeah!
(Looks.)

Gtr. 3

Gtr. 2
divisi

End Rhy. Fig. 6

Guitar Solo

Gtr. 2: w/ Rhy. Fig. 2 (2 times)
Gtr. 4 tacet

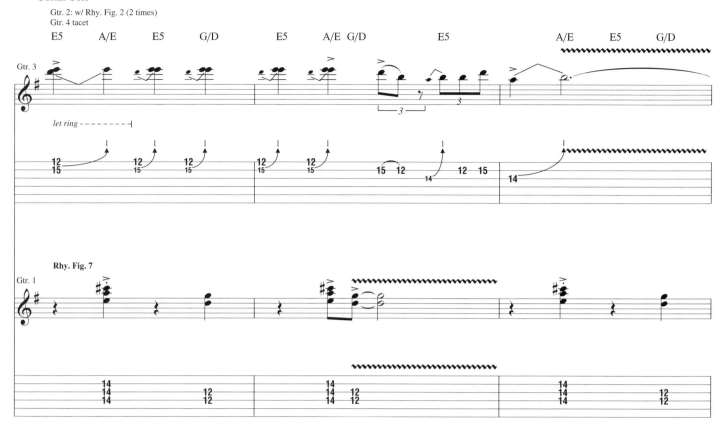

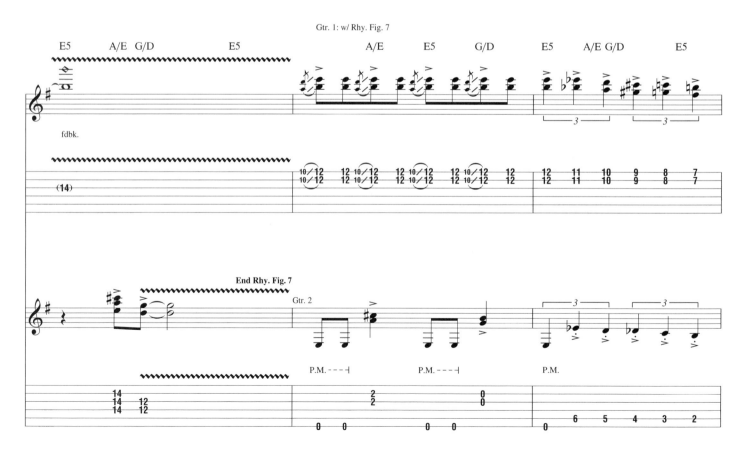

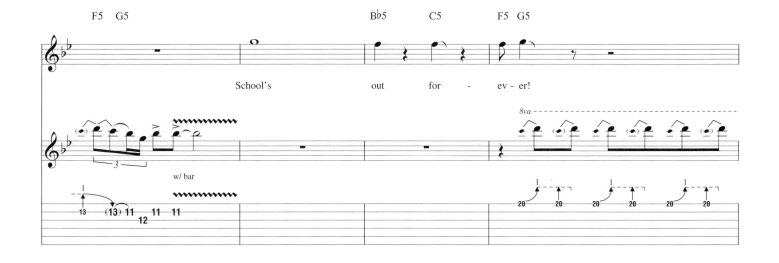

School's out for - ev - er!

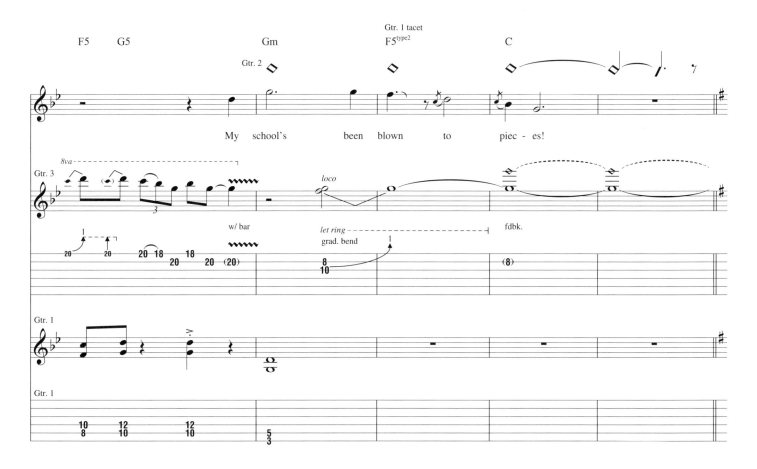

My school's been blown to piec - es!

Bridge

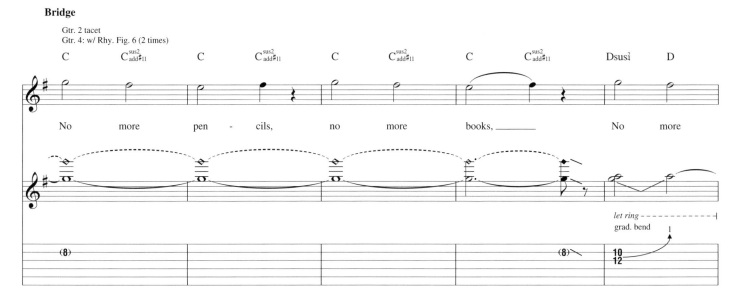

No more pen - cils, no more books, _____ No more

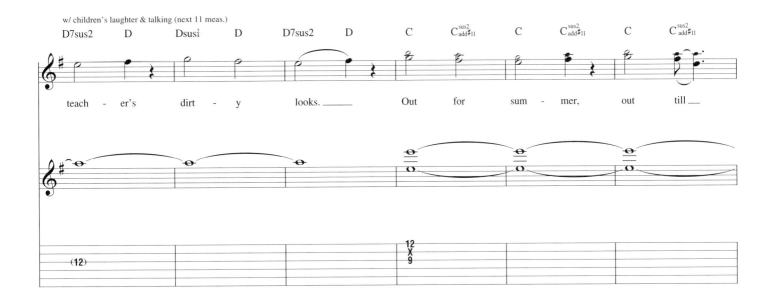

w/ children's laughter & talking (next 11 meas.)

teach - er's dirt - y looks. _____ Out for sum - mer, out till _____

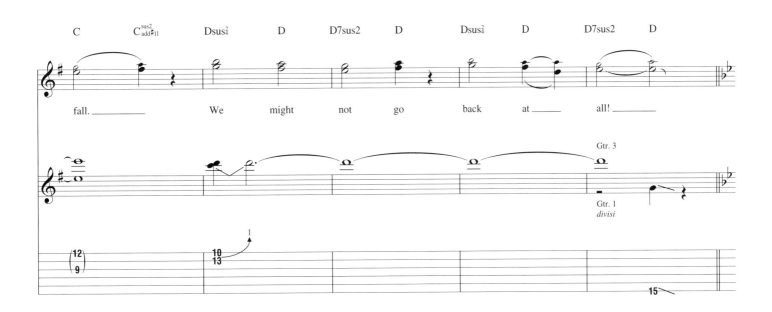

fall. _____ We might not go back at _____ all! _____

Gtr. 3

Gtr. 1
divisi

Outro-Chorus

Gtrs. 1 & 2: w/ Rhy. Figs. 5 & 5A (1 1/2 times)

School's out for - ev - er!
(Out for...)

Gtr. 3

let ring - - -|

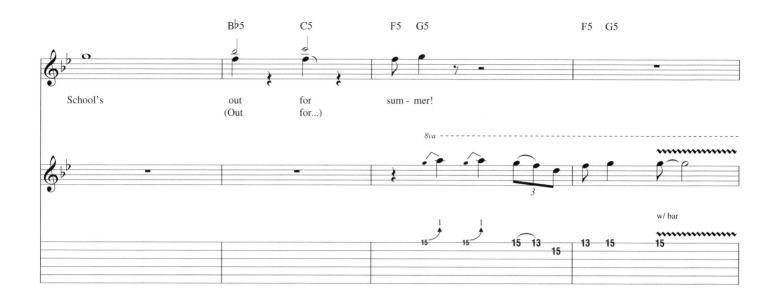

School's out for sum - mer!
(Out for...)

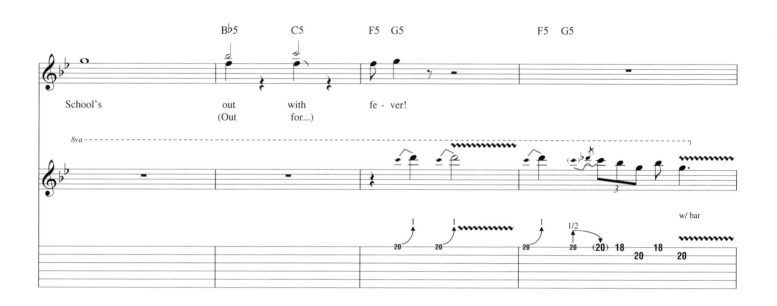

School's out with fe - ver!
(Out for...)

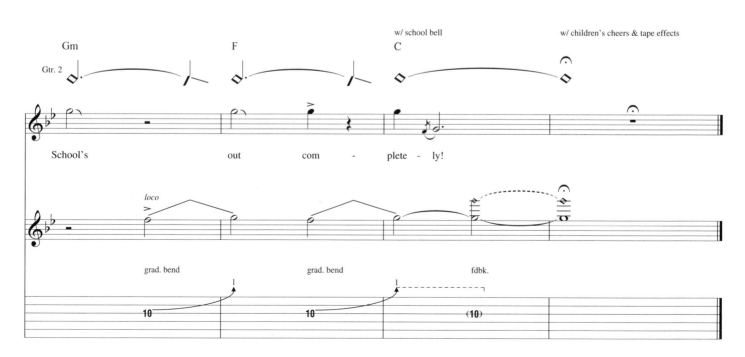

School's out com - plete - ly!

from Mötley Crüe - *Shout at the Devil*

Shout at the Devil

Words and Music by Nikki Sixx

Tune down 1 step:
(low to high) D-G-C-F-A-D

Intro
Moderately ♩ = 94

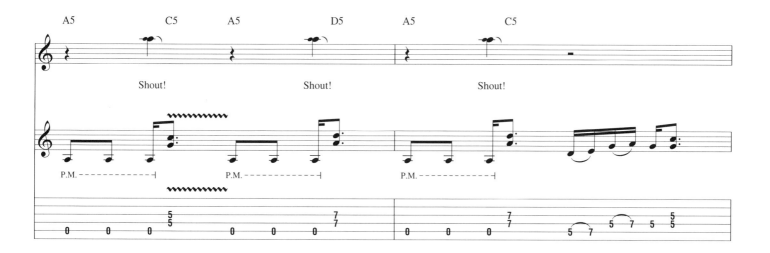

*Gtr. 1 (dist.)

*Doubled throughout

**Chord symbols reflect implied harmony.

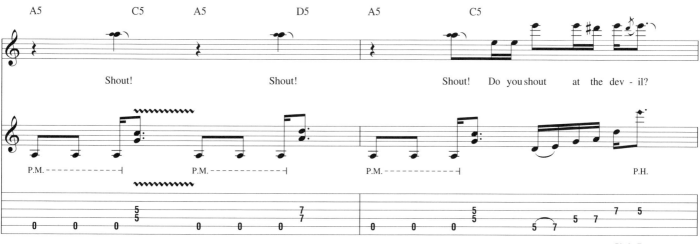

Shout!   Shout!   Shout!

Shout!   Shout!   Shout!   Do you shout   at the dev - il?

Pitch: E

Yeah!

Pitch: E

Verse

He's the wolf scream-in', lone-ly in the night. He's the (1., 3.) blood stain on the stage. _____ He's the

tear in your eye; _ been _ tempt-ed by his lie. He's the knife in your back, he's rage! _ Well, he's the

Verse

Gtr. 1: w/ Riff B

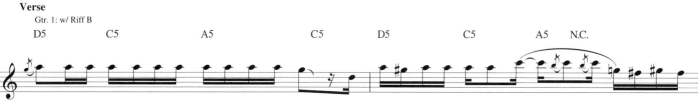

love in your eyes, he'll be the blood be-tween your thighs, and then he'll have you cry for more. _____ He'll put your

strength to the test; he'll put the thrill __ back in bed. __ I'm sure you've heard it all be - fore. __ He'll be the

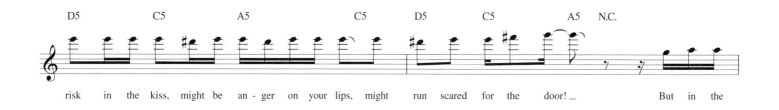

risk in the kiss, might be an - ger on your lips, might run scared for the door! __ But in the

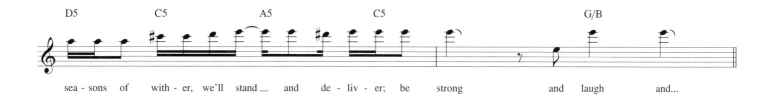

sea - sons of with - er, we'll stand __ and de - liv - er; be strong and laugh and...

Chorus

Gtr. 1: w/ Riff C

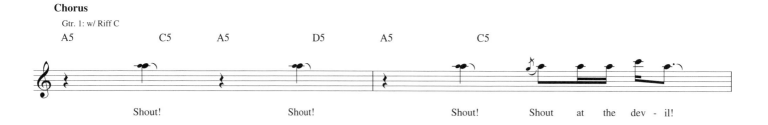

Shout! Shout! Shout! Shout at the dev - il!

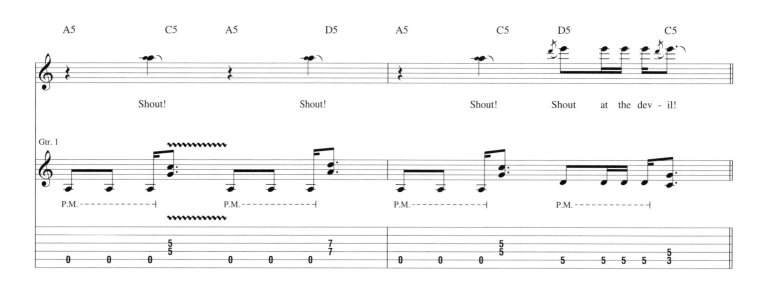

Shout! Shout! Shout! Shout at the dev - il!

P.M. - - - - - - - - - -   P.M. - - - - - - - - - -   P.M. - - - - - - - - - -   P.M. - - - - - - - - -

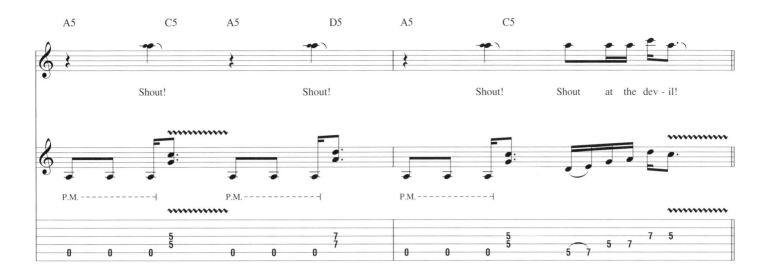

Outro

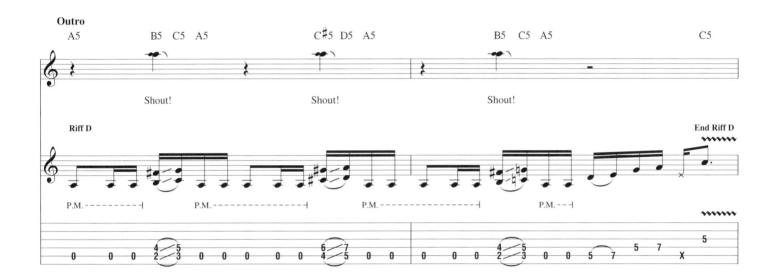

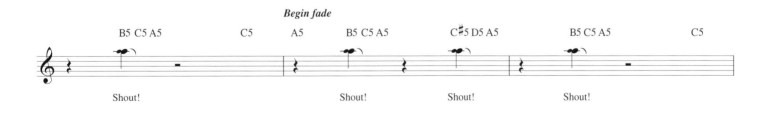

from Deep Purple - *Machine Head*

Smoke on the Water

Words and Music by Ritchie Blackmore, Ian Gillan, Roger Glover, Jon Lord and Ian Paice

A, Frank Zap - pa and the Moth - ers _____ were at the best place a - round. _____
When it all was o - ver, we had to find an - oth - er place. _____
few red lights, a few old beds _ we made a place to sweat. _____

But some stu - pid with a flare gun _ burned the place to the _____ ground. _
But Swiss time was run - ning out; _ it seemed that we would lose the race. _
No mat - ter what we get out of this, I know, I know we'll nev - er for - get.

Chorus

Smoke on the wa - ter, a fire _ in the sky. _

let ring - - - - - - - - - - - -   *let ring - - - - - - - - - - - -*   *let ring - - - - - - - - - - - -*

To Coda ⊕ **Interlude** |1.   Gtr. 1: w/ Riff A (1 3/4 times)   Gtr. 1: w/ Fill 1 |2.   **Interlude**   Gtr. 1: w/ Riff A (1 3/4 times)   Gtr. 1: w/ Fill 1

N.C. (G5)   N.C. (G5)

Smoke on the wa - ter.

let ring - - - - - - - -   *let ring - - - - - - - -*   Gtr. 2 (dist.)

Guitar Solo

Gtr. 2

1/4   1/2

Gtr. 1

slight P.M.   *slight P.M. - - - - - - - - - - - -*

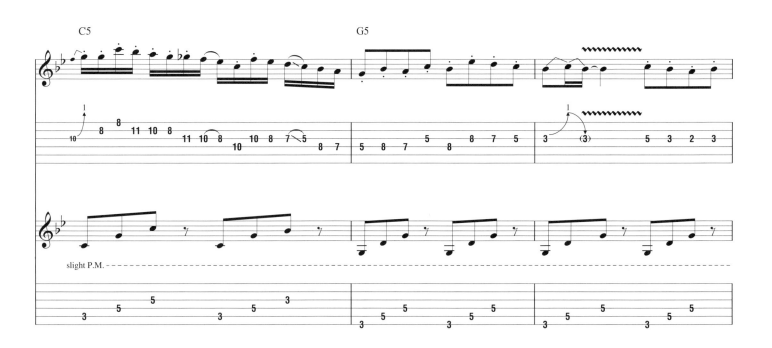

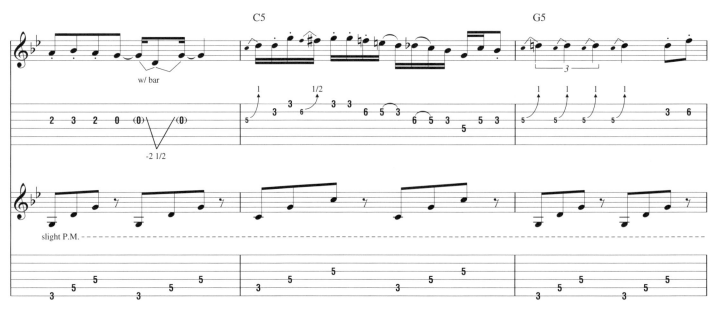

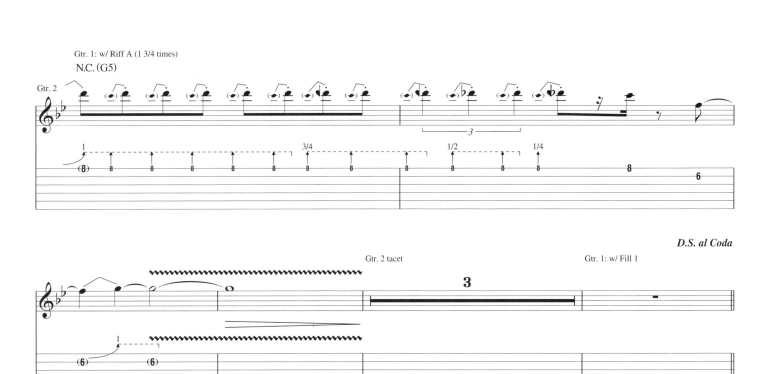

D.S. al Coda

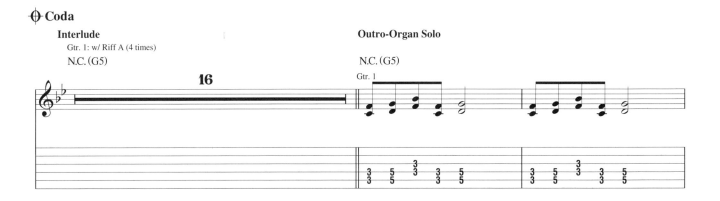

Coda

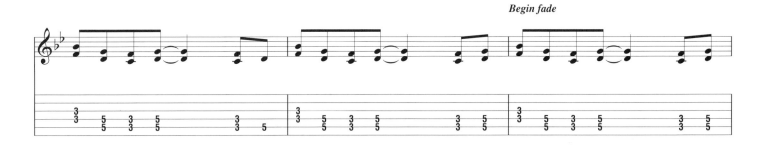

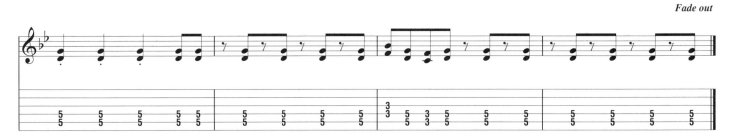

from Whitesnake - *Whitesnake*

Still of the Night

Words and Music by David Coverdale and John Sykes

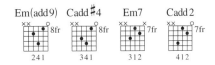

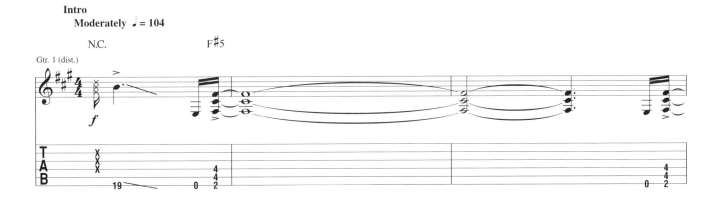

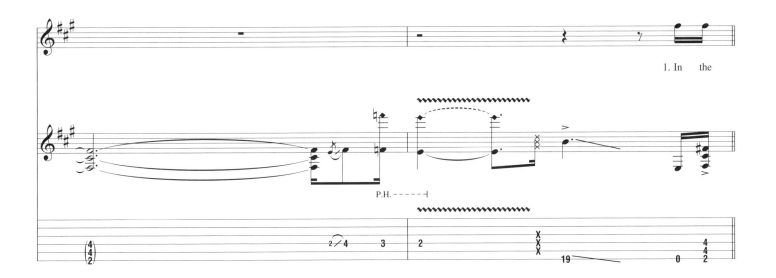

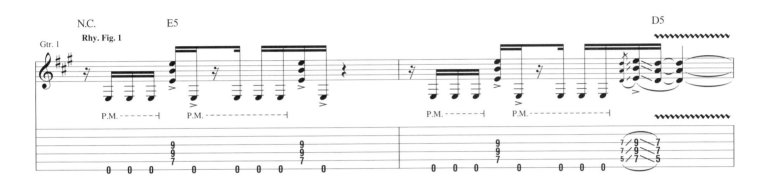

Interlude

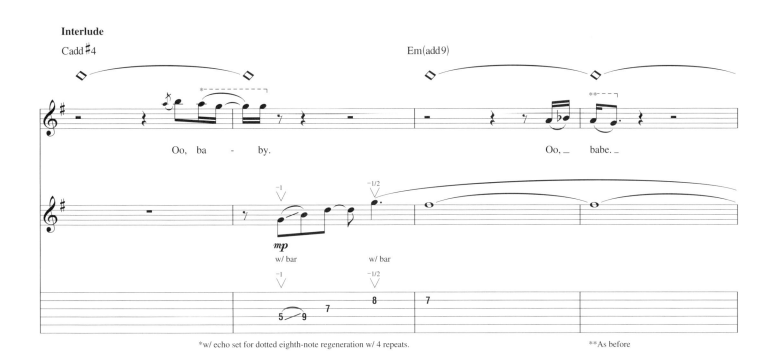

*w/ echo set for dotted eighth-note regeneration w/ 4 repeats.   **As before

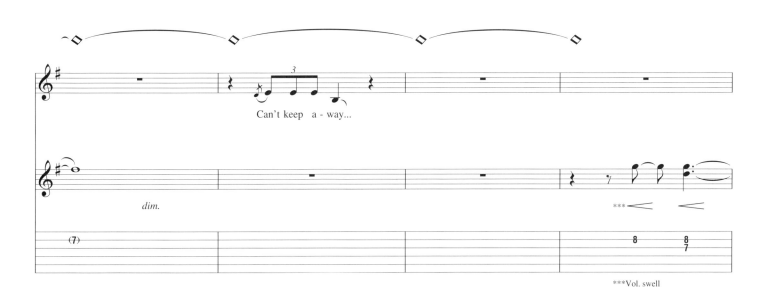

***Vol. swell

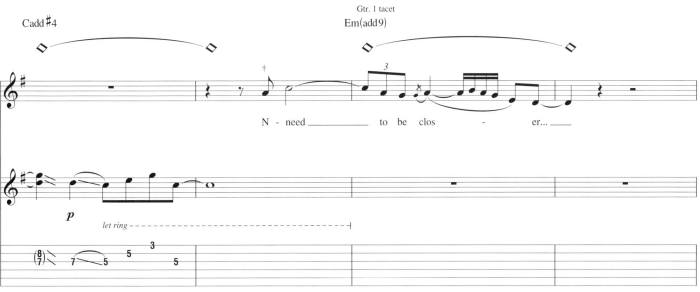

†w/ echo, next 17 meas. (variable rates).

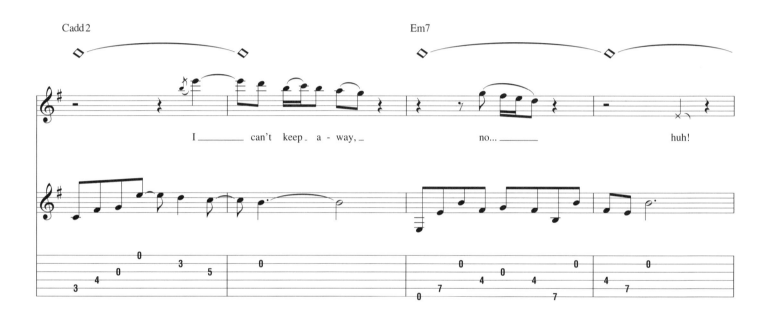

Cadd2   Em7

Can't keep a - way.

Pitch: D   G

Interlude

Gtrs. 3 & 4 tacet

*Em

Riff B   **End Riff B**

Gtr. 5

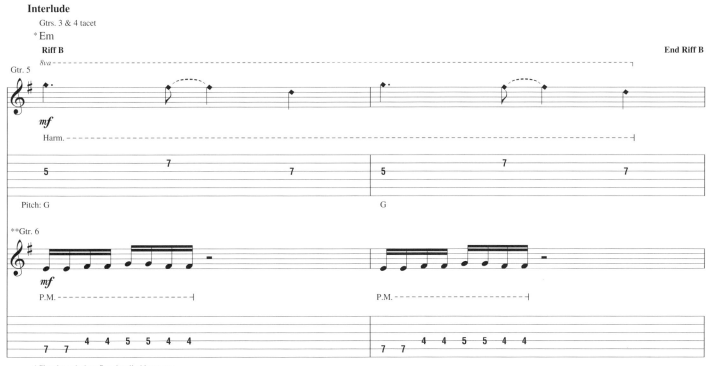

mf

Harm.

Pitch: G   G

**Gtr. 6

mf

P.M.   P.M.

*Chord symbols reflect implied harmony.

**Kybd. arr. for gtr.

Gtr. 5: w/ Riff B (7 times)

C   D

Gtr. 4

loco

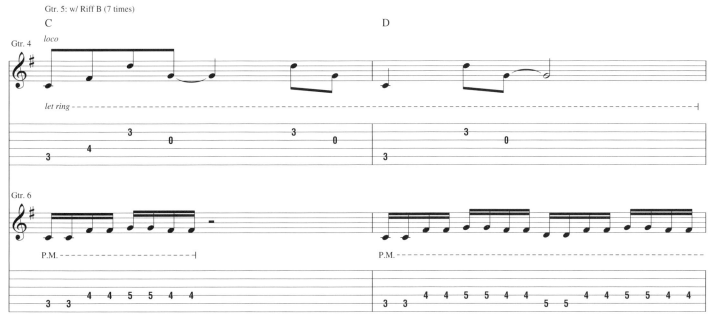

let ring

Gtr. 6

P.M.   P.M.

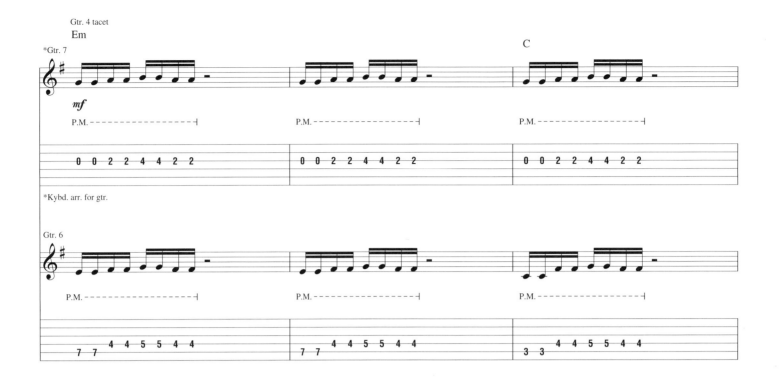

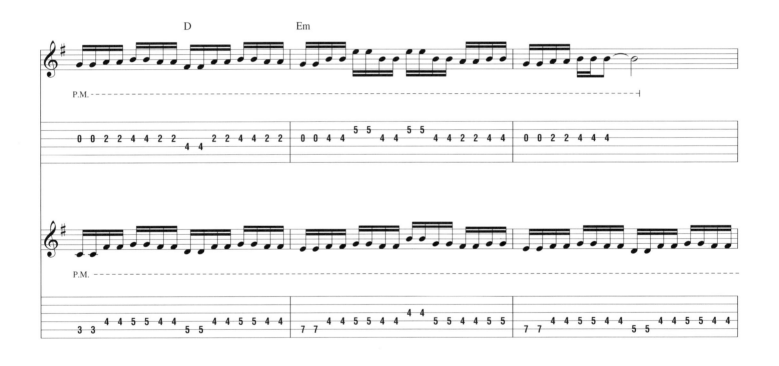

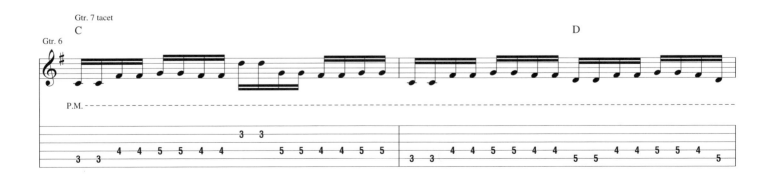

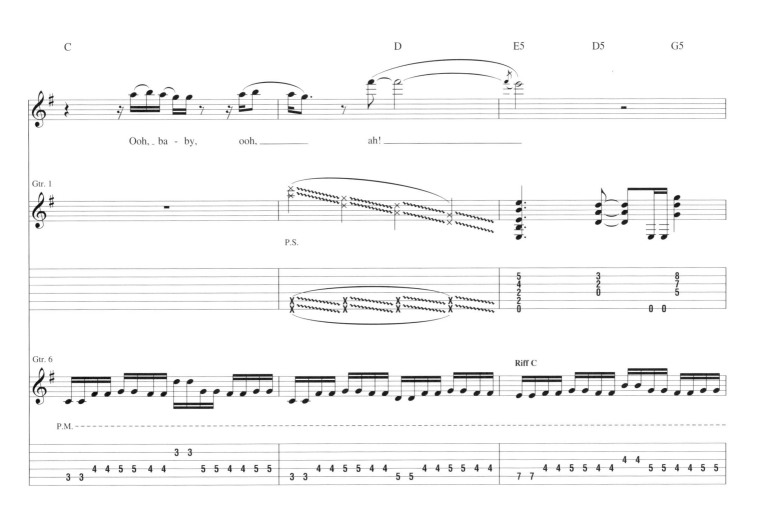

Ooh, ba - by, ooh, _____ ah! _____

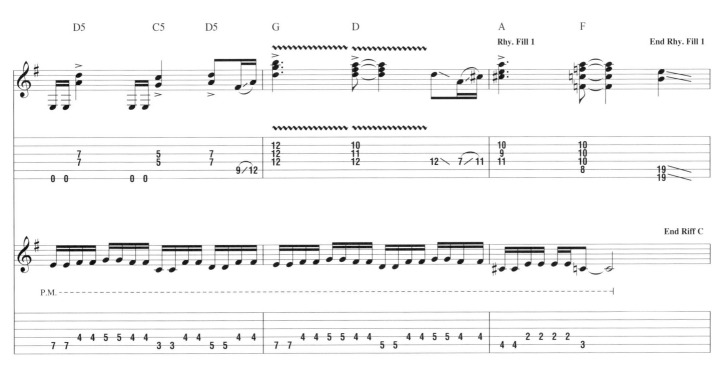

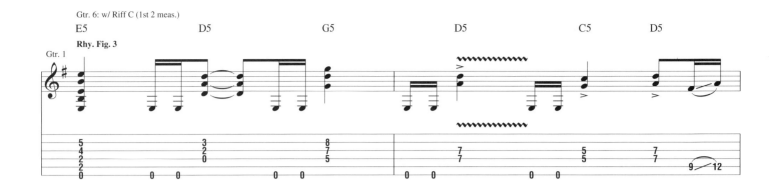

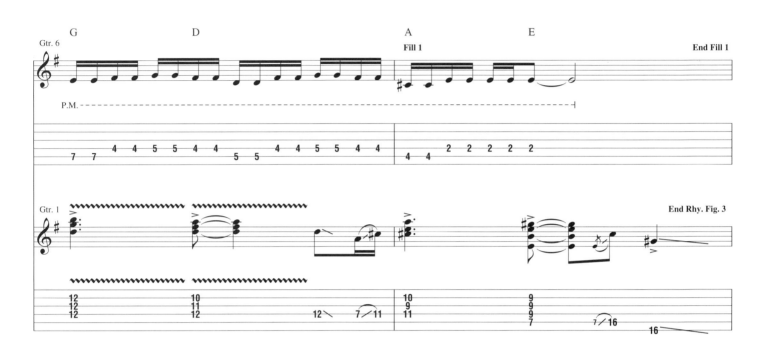

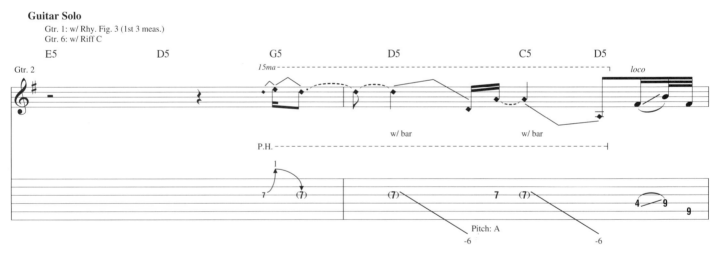

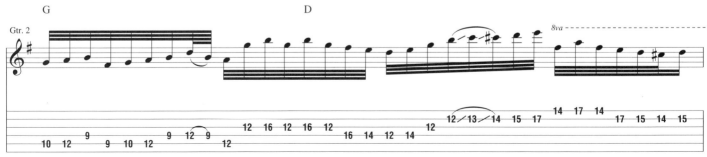

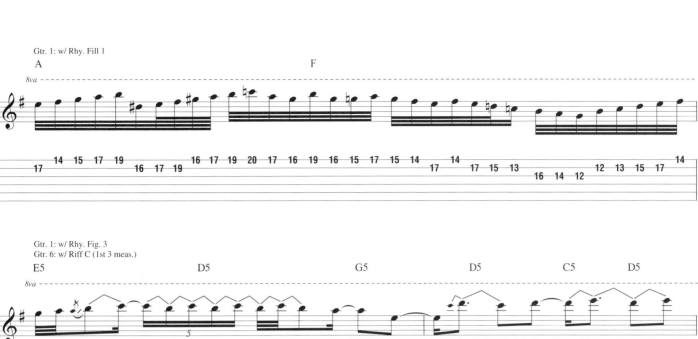

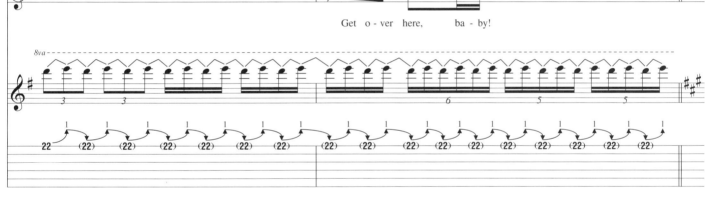

Get o - ver here,   ba - by!

Interlude

Gtr. 2 tacet

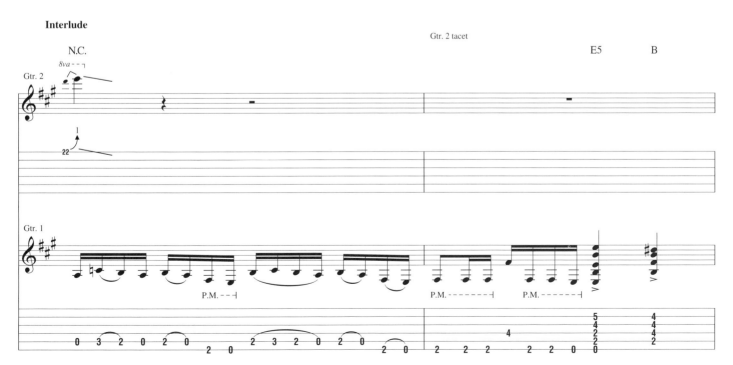

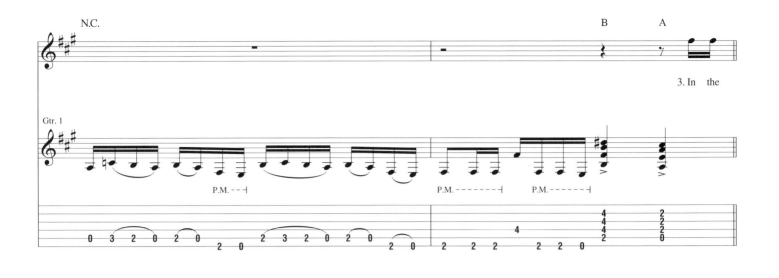

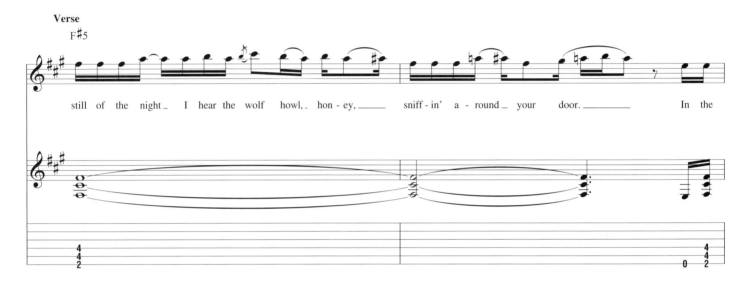

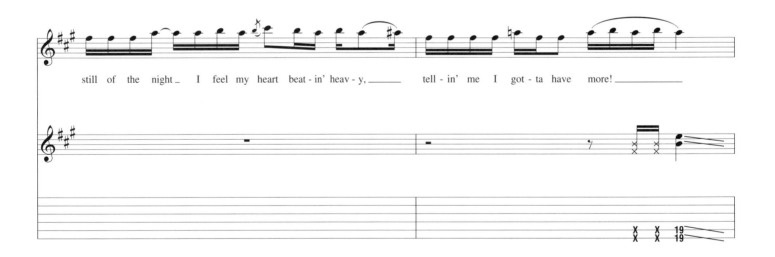

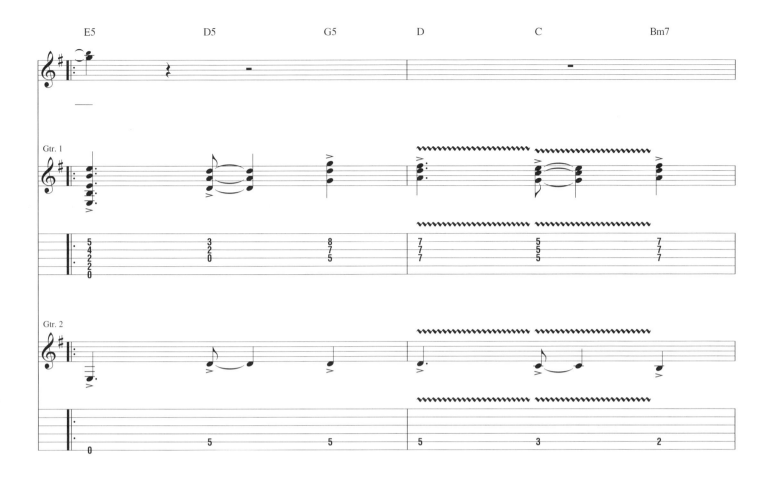

Pre-Chorus
Gtr. 1: w/ Rhy. Fig. 2
D5
A5
Now I just wan-na get close to you an' taste your love so sweet. An'
B5
A5
G
I just wan - na make, a, love to you, feel your bod - y
Fsus2
heat! In the still of the night!
Gtr. 1
P.S.
Outro
E5
D
C
G
A5
G
Oo, yeah!
F
E5
D
C
G
In the still of the night!
I will be sneak - in' 'round your door.
let ring

Play 4 times & fade

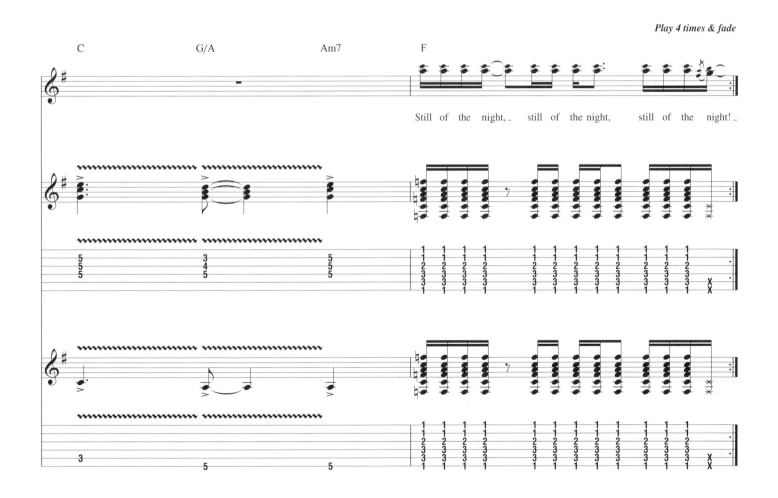

Still of the night, _ still of the night, still of the night! _

from Rainbow - *Straight Between the Eyes*

Stone Cold

Words by Roger Glover and Joe Lynn Turner
Music by Ritchie Blackmore

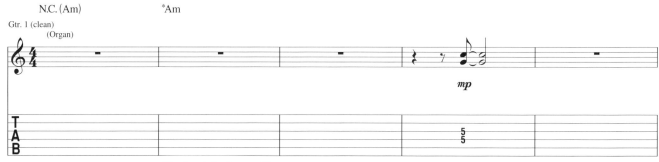

*Chord symbols reflect overall harmony.

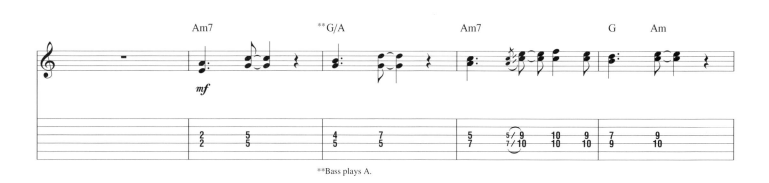

**Bass plays A.

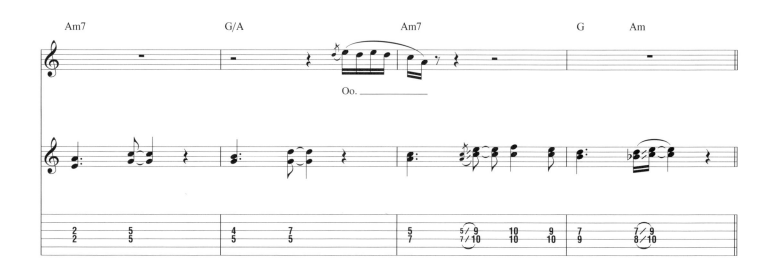

Verse

1. Ev-'ry night I have the same old dream, 'bout you and me and what's in be-tween.

So man-y chang-es, so man-y lies.

Try to run,   try to hide   from ev-'ry-thing that I feel___ in - side___ but I can't___

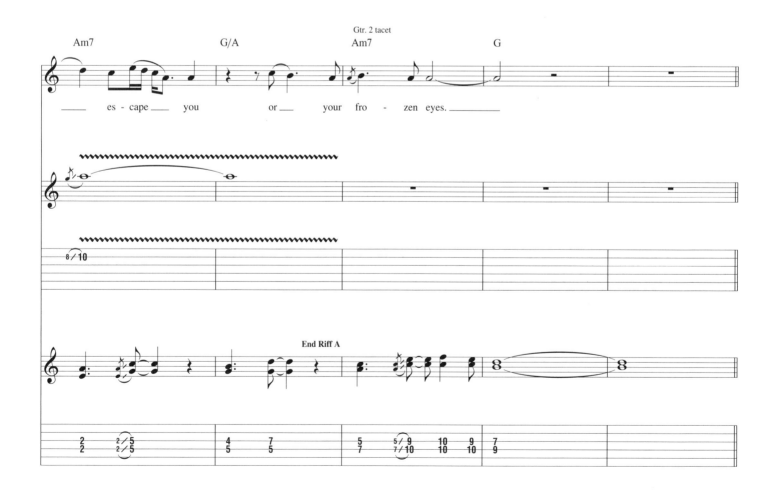

es - cape___ you   or___ your fro - zen eyes.___

Pre-Chorus

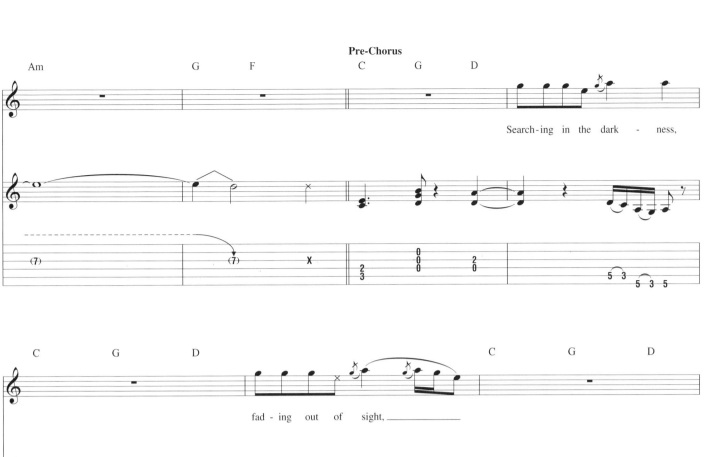

Search-ing in the dark - ness,

fad - ing out of sight, _____

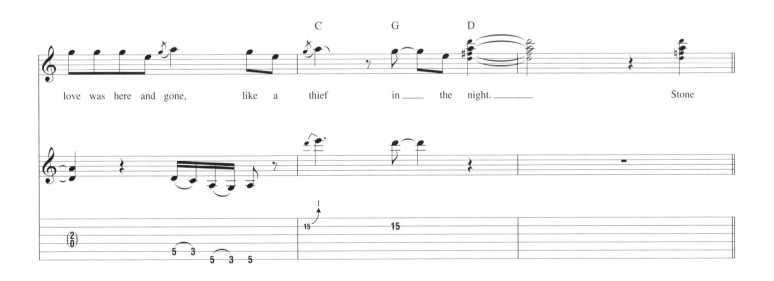

love was here and gone, like a thief in ___ the night. _____ Stone

Chorus

Gtr. 3: w/ Riff B (4 times)

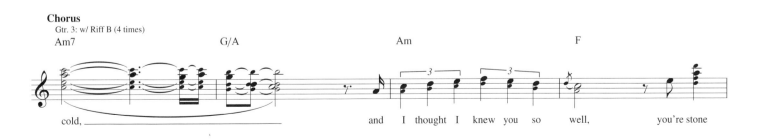

cold, _____ and I thought I knew you so well, you're stone

169

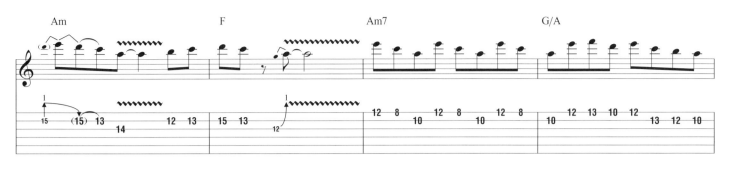

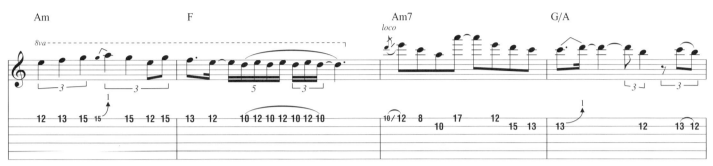

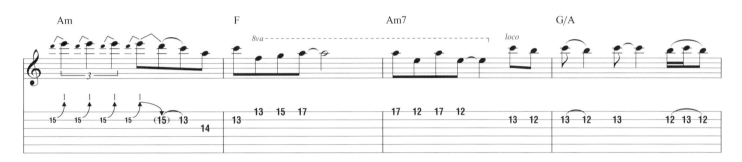

Begin fade

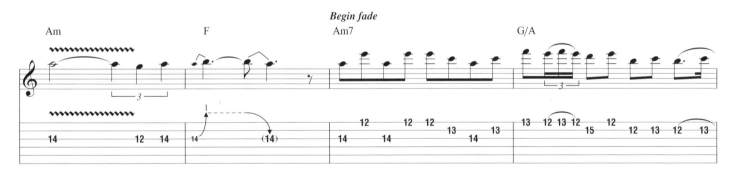

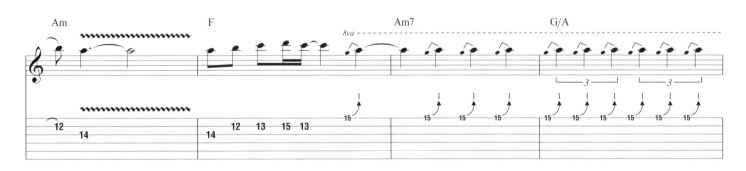

Fade out

from Guns N' Roses - *Appetite for Destruction*

Welcome to the Jungle

Words and Music by W. Axl Rose, Slash, Izzy Stradlin', Duff McKagan and Steven Adler

Tune down 1/2 step:
(low to high) E♭-A♭-D♭-G♭-B♭-E♭

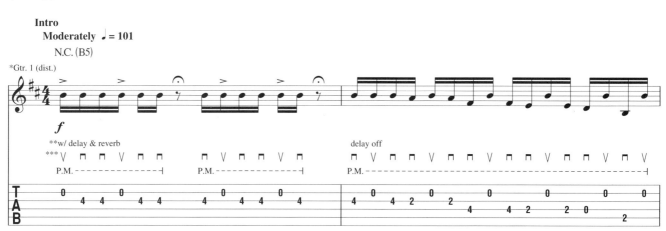

*Slash **Set delay for dotted eighth-note regeneration w/ 2 repeats.
***∨ = upstroke; ⊓ = downstroke

†††Second string open is played with an upstroke, other notes are played with downstrokes.

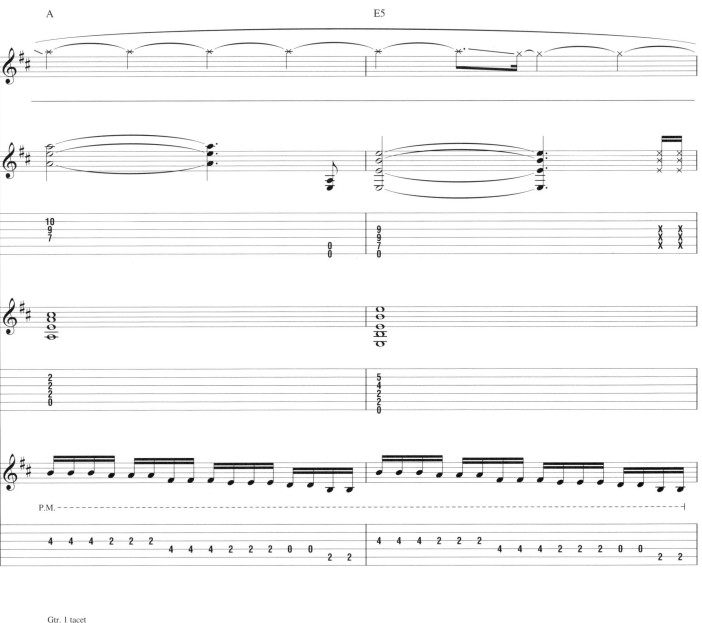

Gtr. 1 tacet

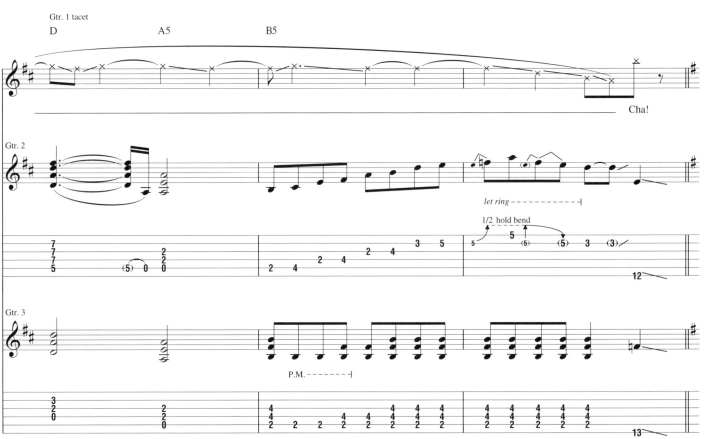

*Chord symbols reflect overall harmony.

Pitch: A

1. Wel-come to the jun - gle, we got fun 'n' games. _____

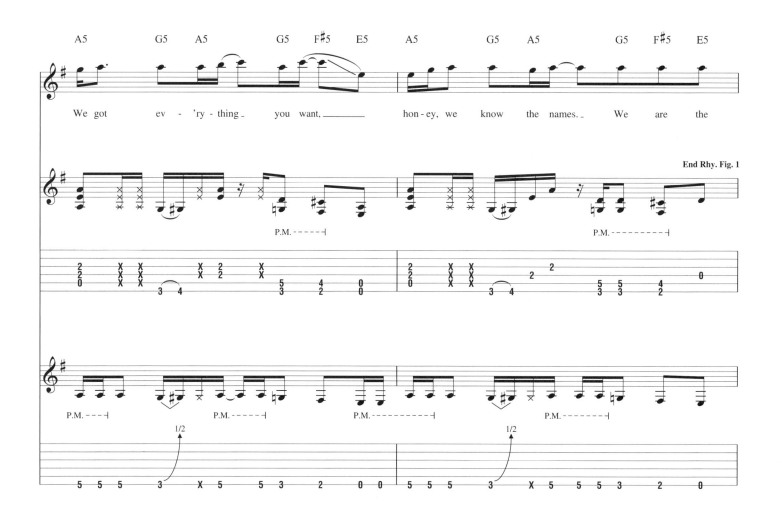

We got ev - 'ry - thing_ you want,_____ hon - ey, we know the names._ We are the

End Rhy. Fig. 1

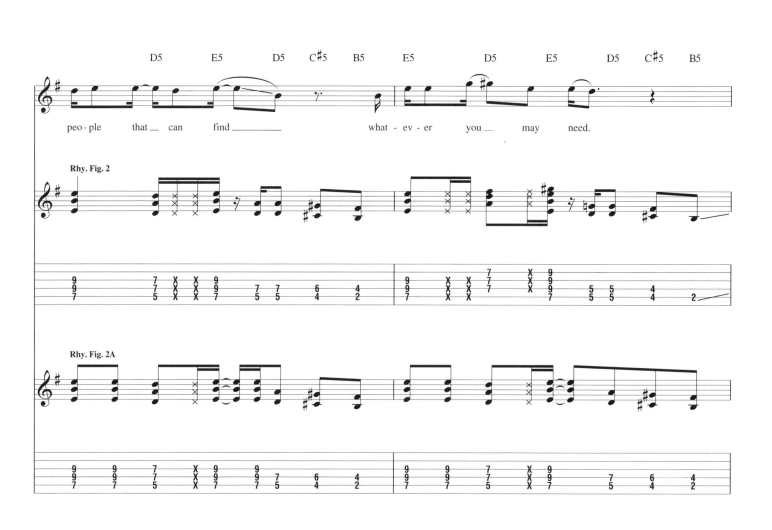

peo - ple that_ can find _____ what - ev - er you_ may need.

Rhy. Fig. 2

Rhy. Fig. 2A

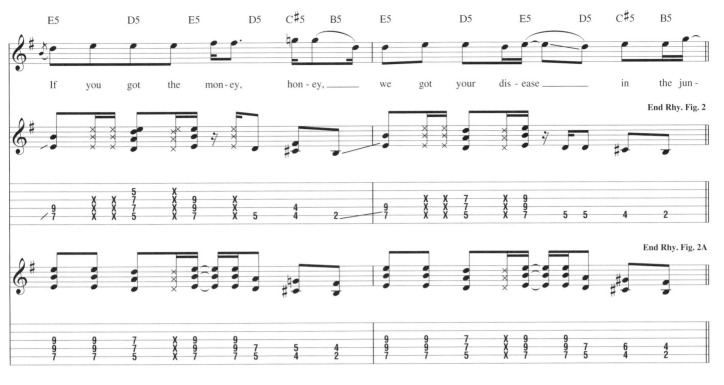

If you got the mon-ey, hon-ey, _____ we got your dis-ease _____ in the jun-

End Rhy. Fig. 2

End Rhy. Fig. 2A

Chorus

- gle. Wel-come to the jun - gle, watch it bring you to your,

Voc. Fig. 1

End Voc. Fig. 1

(Ah, _____ ah.) _____

Gtr. 4 (dist.)

Fill 1

End Fill 1

f
*w/ delay

*Set for quarter-note regeneration w/ 2 repeats.

Riff A

End Riff A

Gtr. 2

Gtr. 3

P.M. - - - ┘   P.M. - - - ┘

Guitar Solo

E7

Gtr. 3: w/ Rhy. Fig. 3 (2 times)

Oh, _____ oh. _____

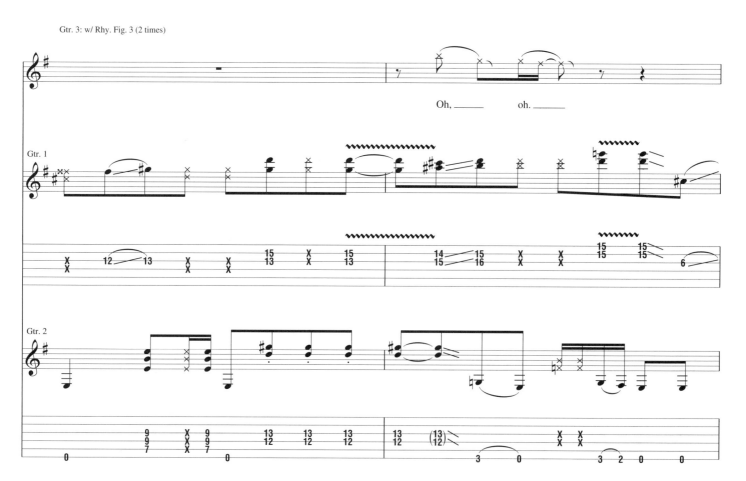

Uh,   uh,   uh,

D5   D#5   E5   D5   D#5   E5   D5   D#5   E5   D5   D#5   E5

uh,   uh,   uh,   uh.

Gtr. 1

15ma   loco

P.H.

Rhy. Fig. 4   End Rhy. Fig. 4

Gtr. 3

P.M. - - - - - ⌐   P.M.

Gtr. 2

Interlude

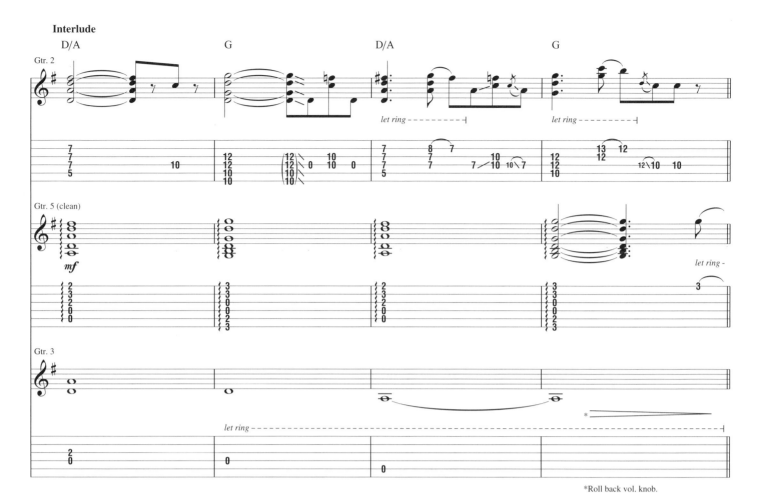

*Roll back vol. knob.

Bridge

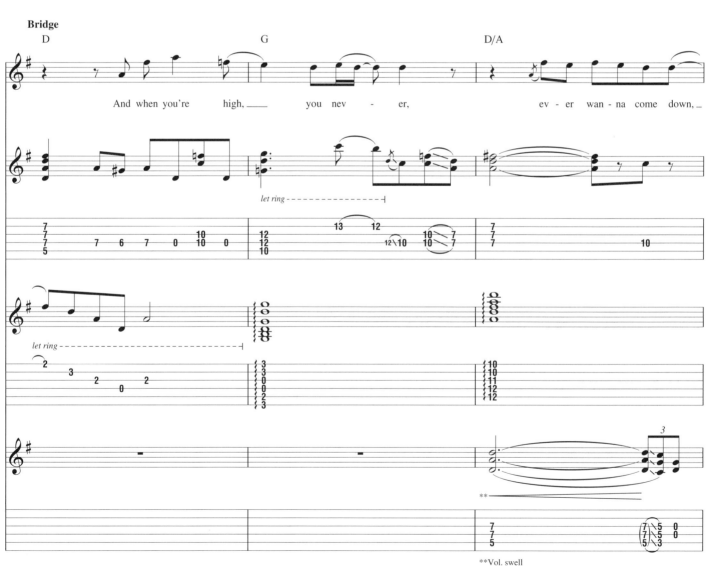

And when you're high, ___ you nev - er, ev - er wan - na come down, ___

**Vol. swell

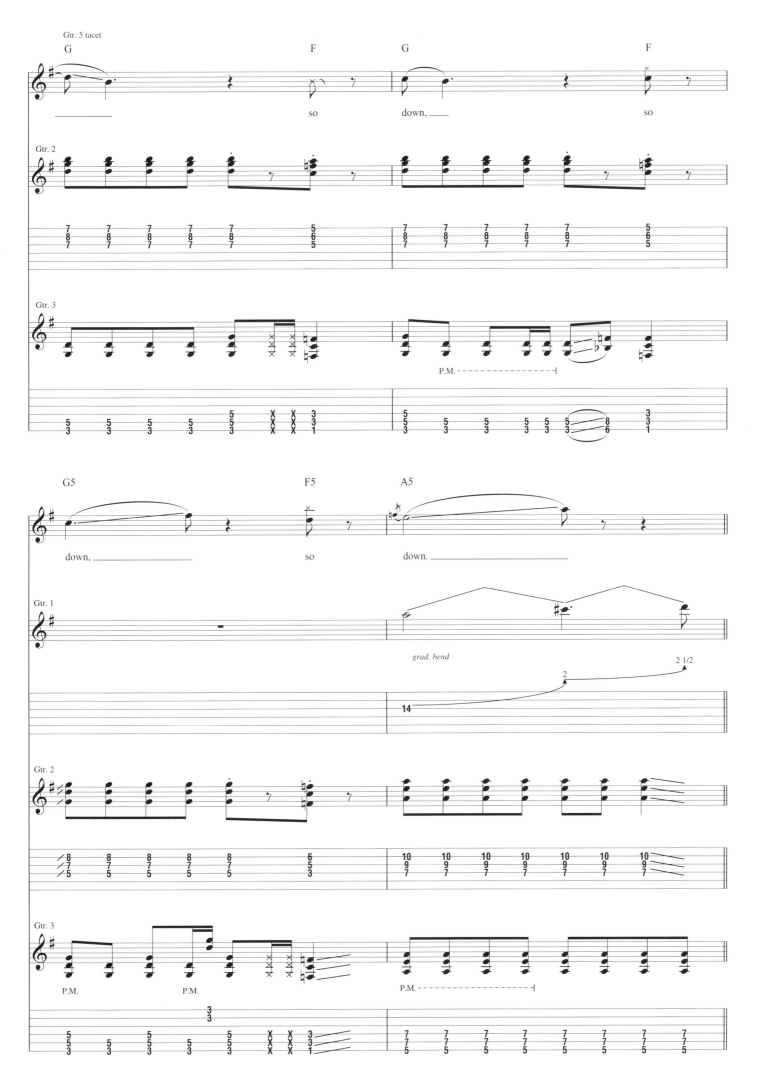

Guitar Solo

Gtr. 3: w/ Rhy. Fig. 3

E7

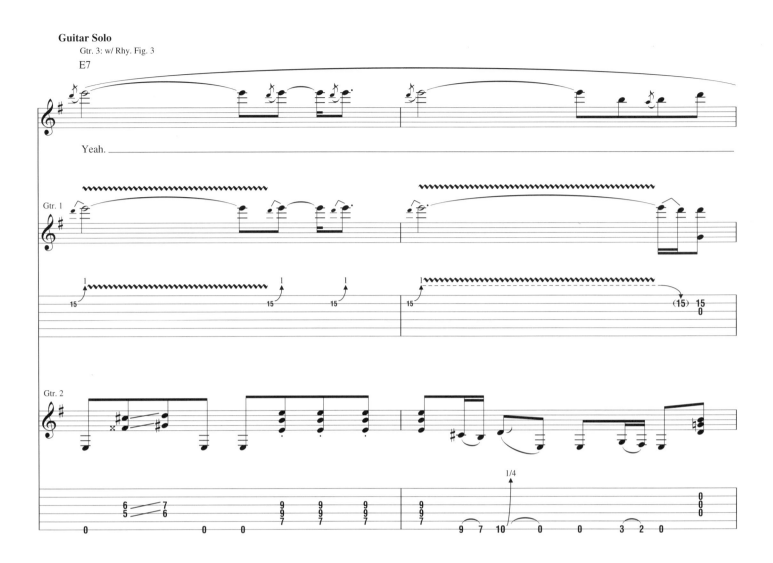

Yeah. _____

Gtr. 1

Gtr. 2

Gtr. 3: w/ Rhy. Fig. 4

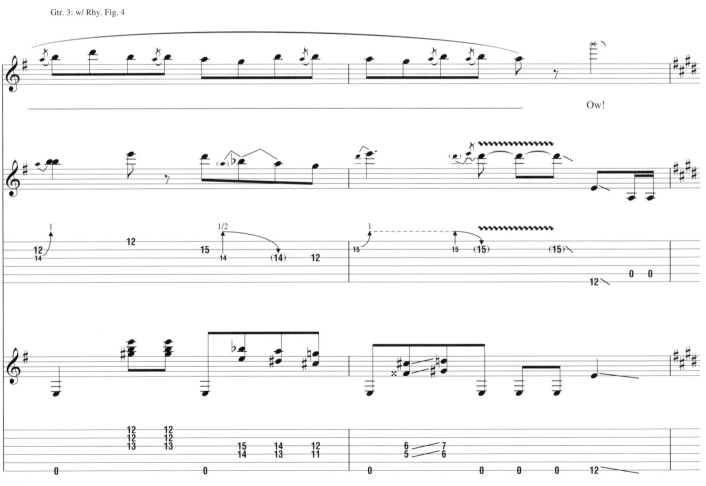

Ow!

*Hypothetical frets; located over pickups

You know_ where you are?_____ You're in the jun - gle, ba - by.

It's ___ gon - na ___ bring you down! _____ Huh!

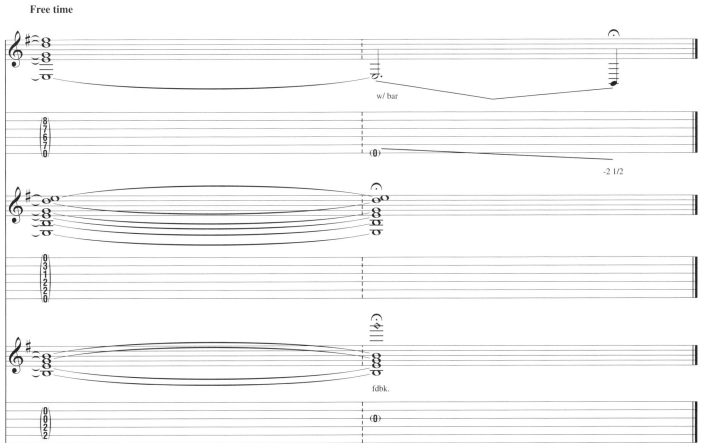

Free time

Whole Lotta Love

Words and Music by Jimmy Page, Robert Plant, John Paul Jones, John Bonham and Willie Dixon

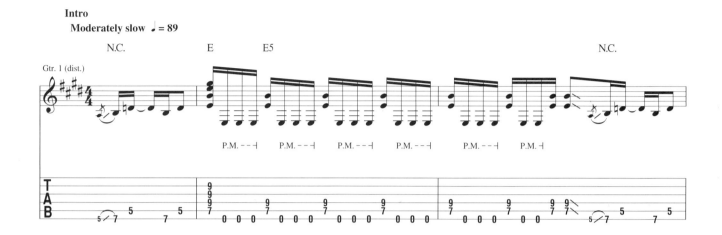

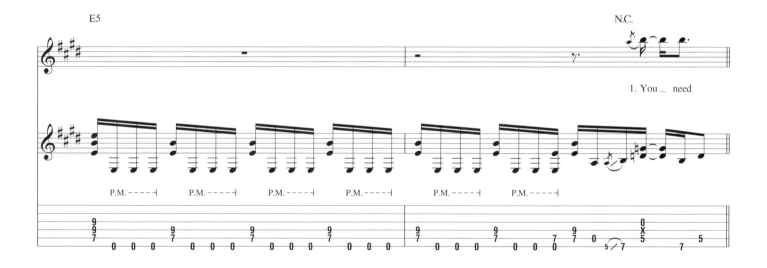

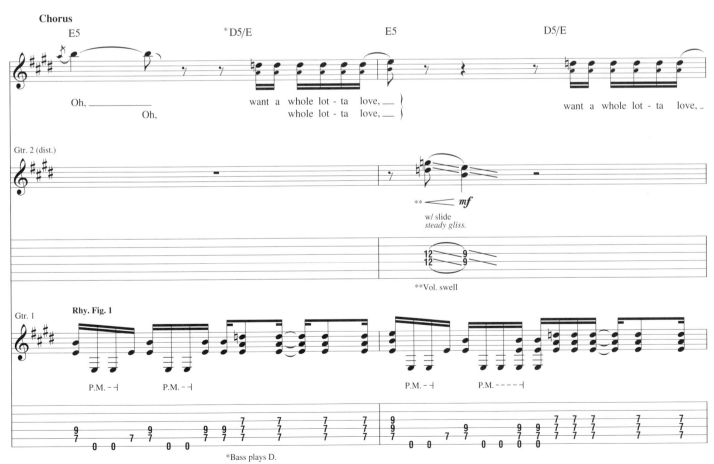

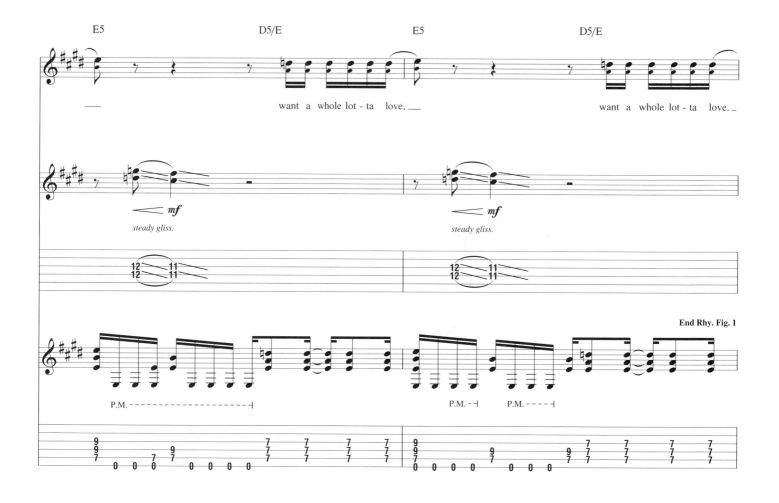

want a whole lot-ta love, ___   want a whole lot-ta love. _

steady gliss.   *steady gliss.*

End Rhy. Fig. 1

P.M.   P.M.   P.M.

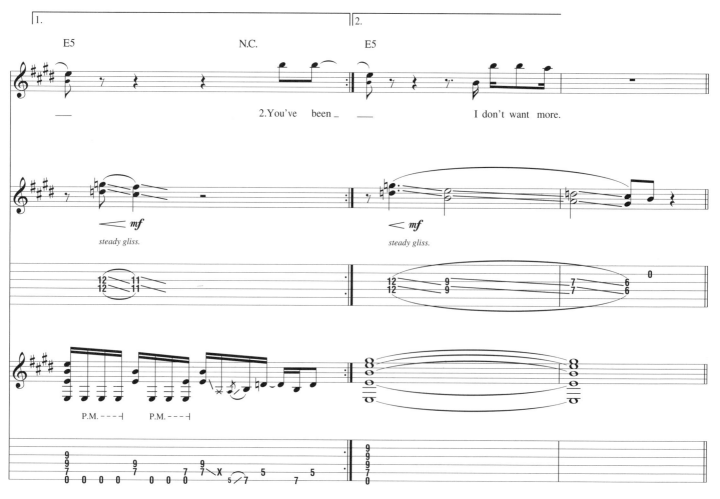

2.You've been _ ___   I don't want more.

steady gliss.   *steady gliss.*

P.M.   P.M.

Interlude

Gtrs. 1 & 2 tacet

w/ misc. gtr. effects, theremin & voc. ad libs.

N.C.

(drums & perc.) **7** **29** (drum fill)

Guitar Solo

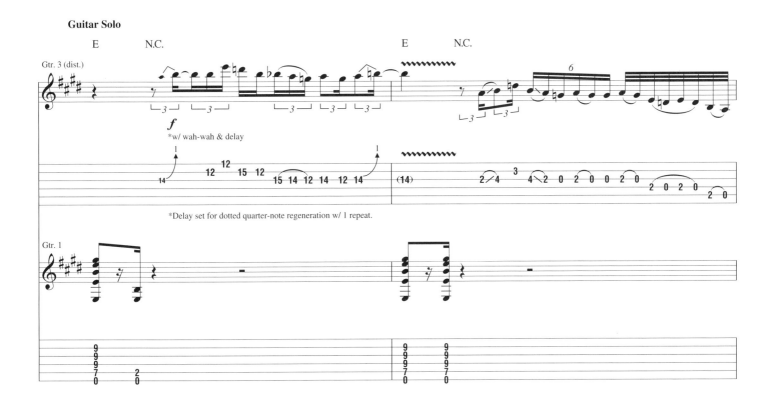

*w/ wah-wah & delay

*Delay set for dotted quarter-note regeneration w/ 1 repeat.

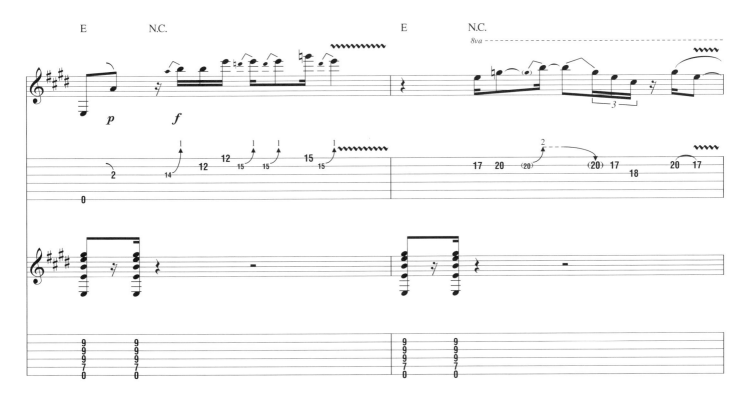

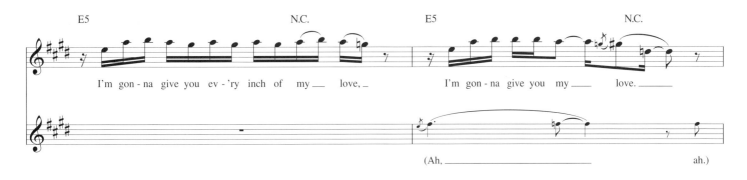

I'm gon-na give you ev-'ry inch of my ___ love, ___ I'm gon-na give you my ___ love. ___

(Ah, _____ ah.)

Yeah, ___ al - right, ___ let's go!

P.M. --- P.M. --- P.M. -- P.M.

Chorus

Gtr. 1: w/ Rhy. Fig. 1

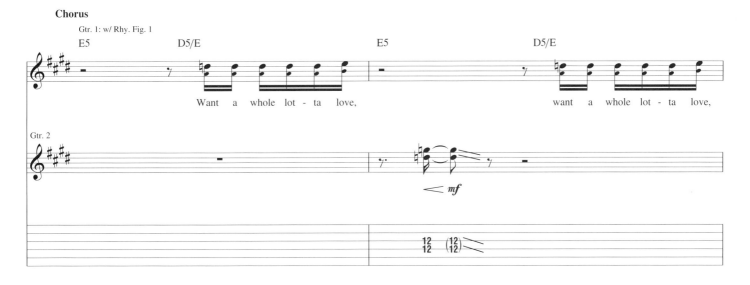

Want a whole lot - ta love, want a whole lot - ta love,

Gtr. 2

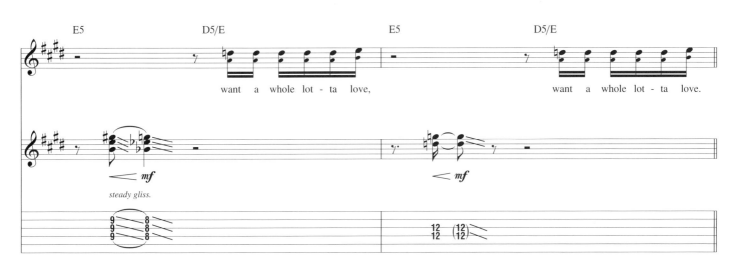

want a whole lot - ta love, want a whole lot - ta love.

steady gliss.

Interlude

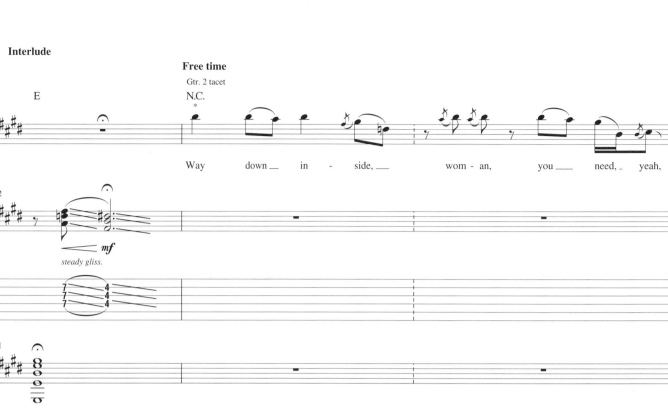

Way down ___ in - side, ___ wom - an, you ___ need, ___ yeah,

*w/ vocal bleed-through from previously recorded
vocal track w/ ambient echo, next 2 meas.

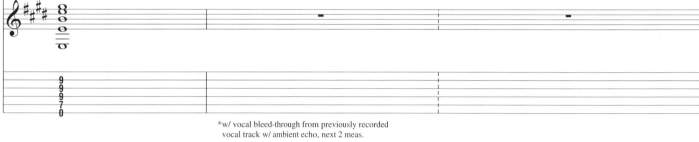

love. _____

**w/ echo, next 3 meas.

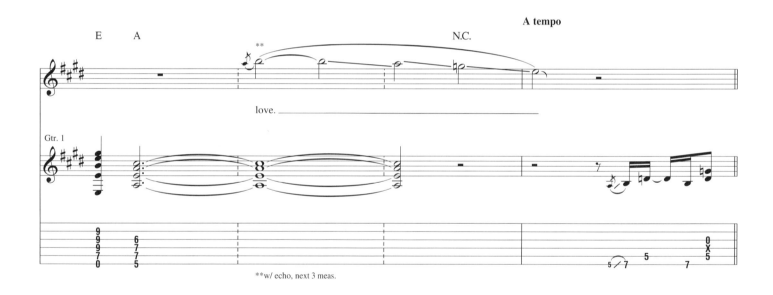

Outro

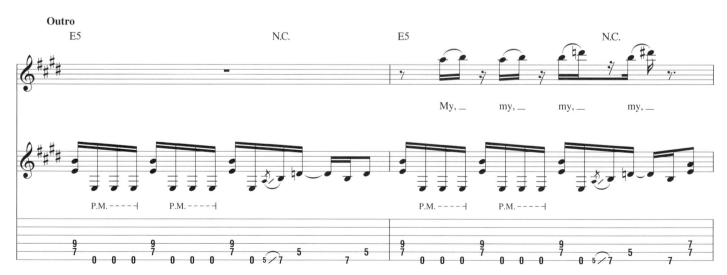

My, ___ my, ___ my, ___ my, ___

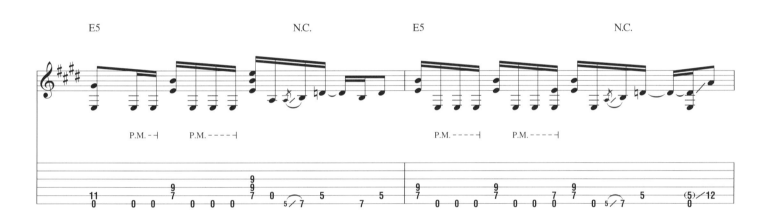

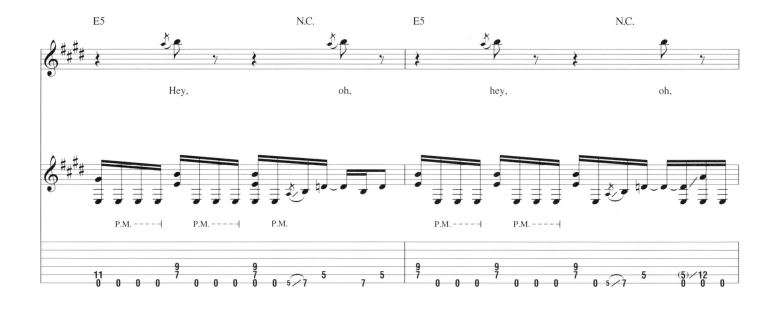

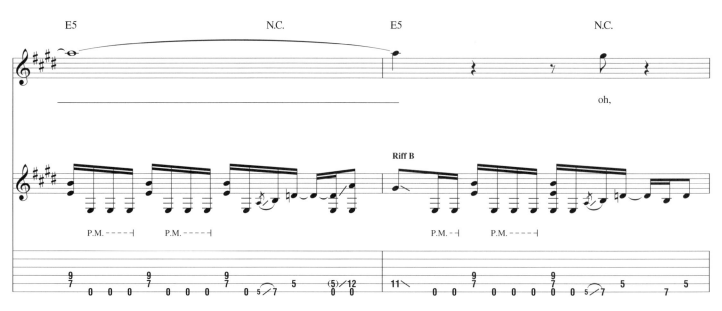

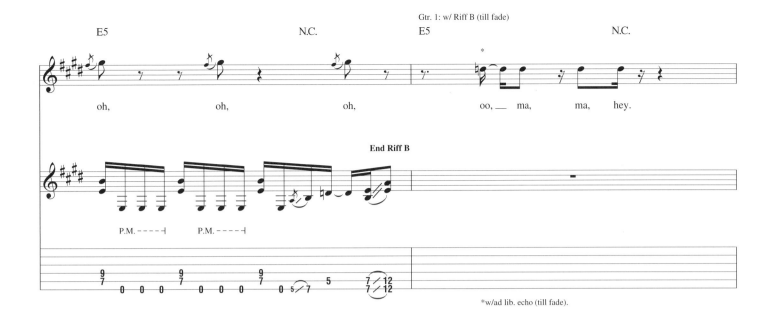

Gtr. 1: w/ Riff B (till fade)

oh,   oh,   oh,   oo, __ ma,   ma, hey.

End Riff B

P.M. - - - -| P.M. - - - -|

*w/ad lib. echo (till fade).

Keep it cool - in', ba - by,

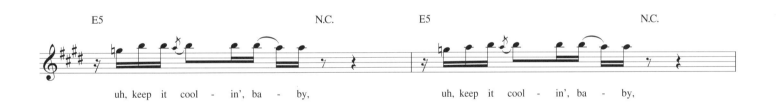

uh, keep it cool - in', ba - by,   uh, keep it cool - in', ba - by,

Begin fade

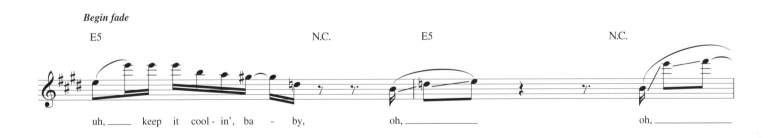

uh, ___ keep it cool - in', ba - by,   oh, _____   oh, _____

Fade out

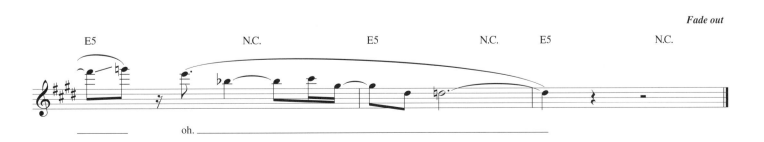

___ oh. _____

from Rush - *Rush*

Working Man

Words and Music by Geddy Lee and Alex Lifeson

Chorus

Well, they call me the work - in' man, I guess _ that's what I

Intro
Double time ♩ = 156

am.

Guitar Solo

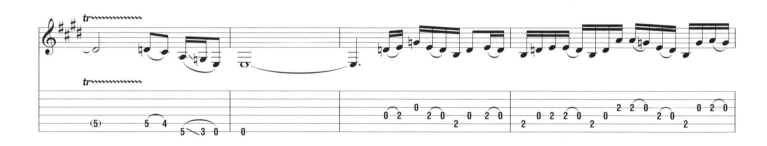

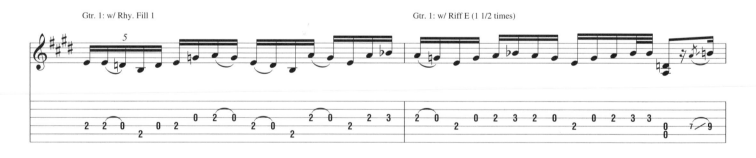

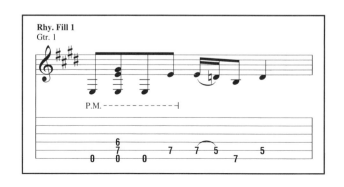

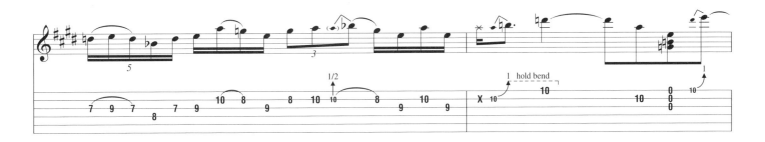

Gtr. 1: w/ Rhy. Fill 2

Gtr. 1: w/ Riff E (1 1/2 times)

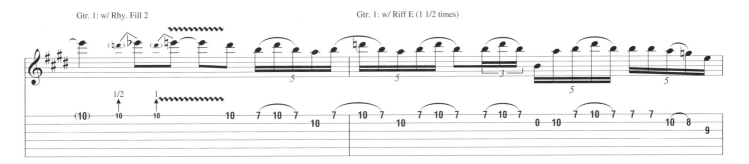

Gtr. 1: w/ Rhy. Fill 3

Gtr. 1: w/ Riff E (1 1/2 times)

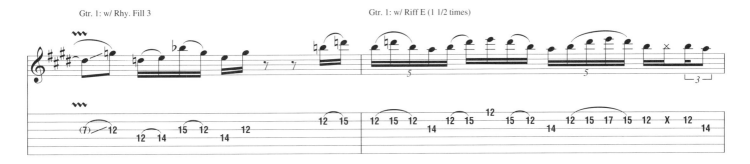

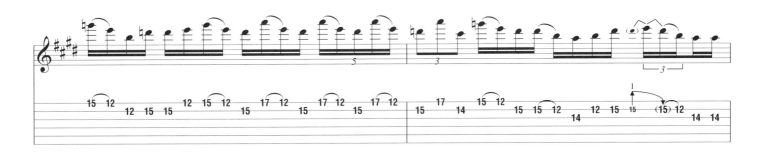

Rhy. Fill 2
Gtr. 1

Rhy. Fill 3
Gtr. 1

Gtr. 1: w/ Riff E (4 times)

Gtr. 2

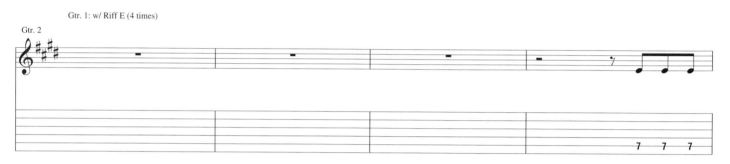

Gtr. 2

Gtr. 1   Riff G

End Riff G

P.M. -

Pitch: G#   D#

P.H.   P.H.

Gtr. 1: w/ Riff G (3 times)

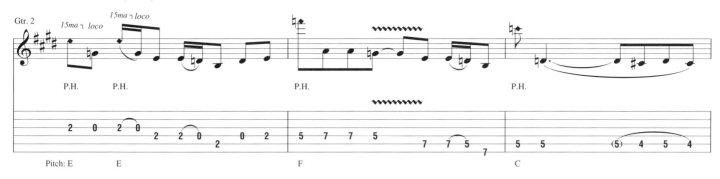

Gtr. 1: w/ Riff E (1 1/2 times)

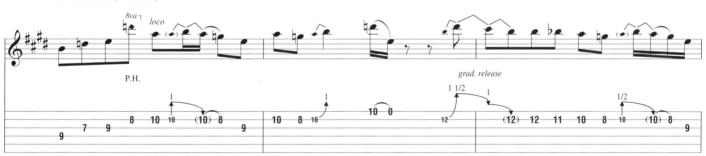

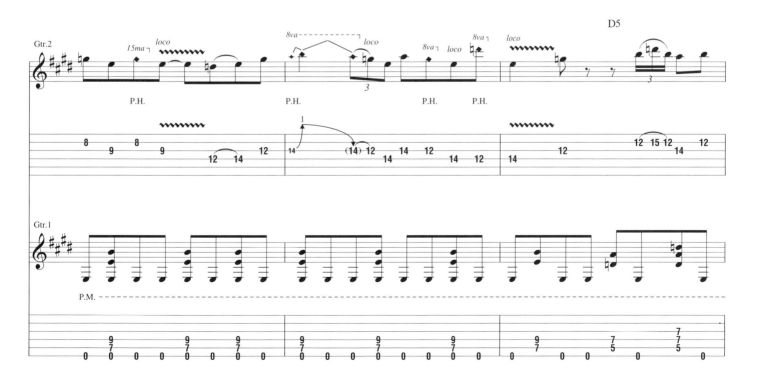

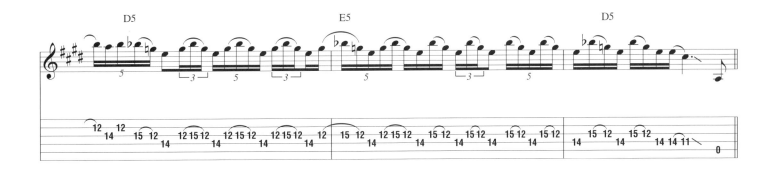

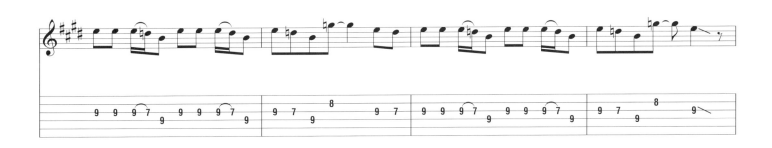

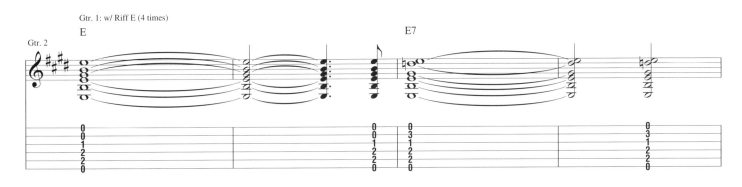

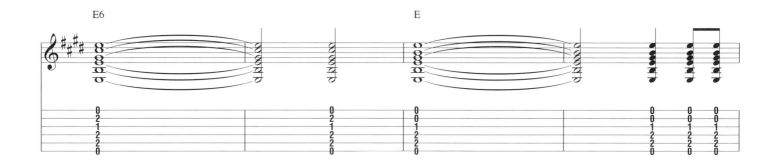

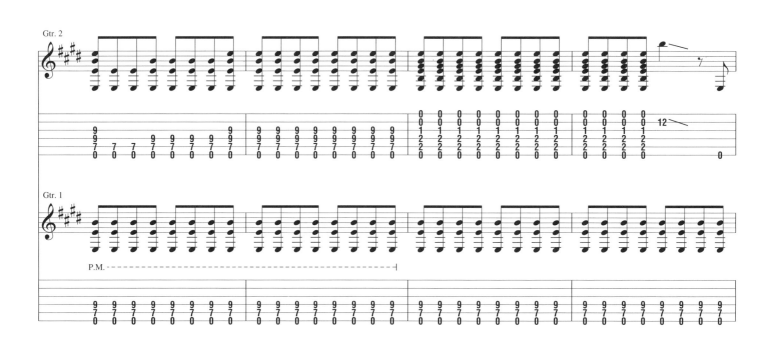

Outro
Slower ♩ = 70

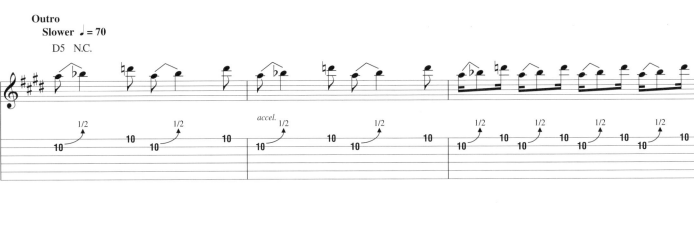

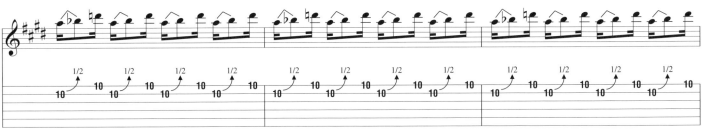

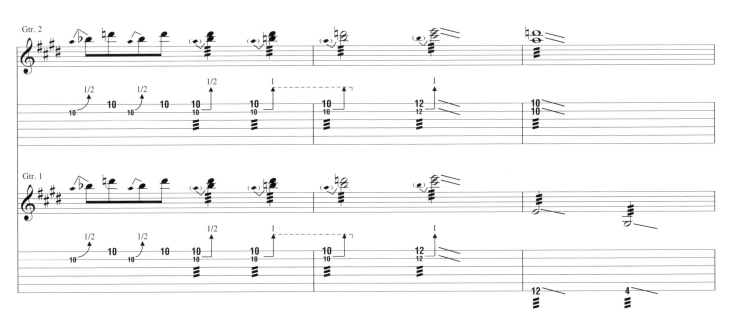

Free time

You've Got Another Thing Comin'

Words and Music by Glenn Tipton, Rob Halford and K.K. Downing

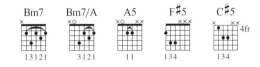

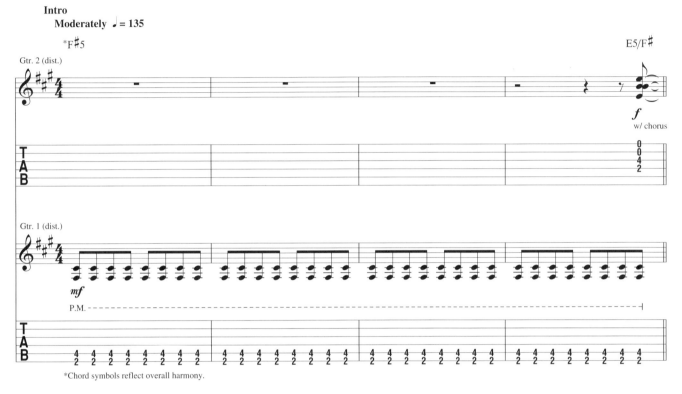

*Chord symbols reflect overall harmony.

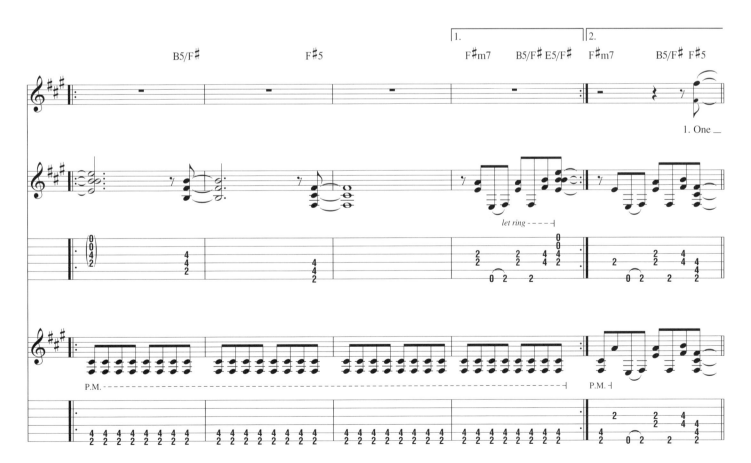

You've got an-oth-er thing com-in'.

In this world we're liv-in' in __ we __ have __ our share __ of sor-row. An-

*See top of first page of song for chord diagrams pertaining to rhythm slashes.

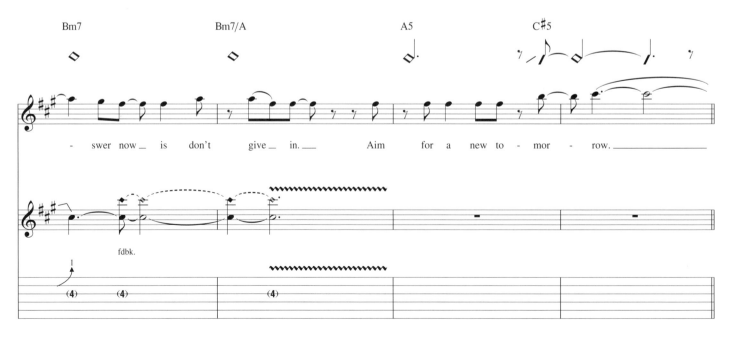

-swer now __ is don't give __ in. __ Aim for a new to-mor-row. _____

Guitar Solo

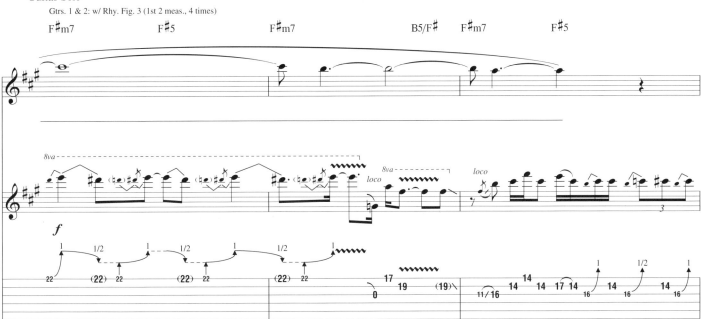

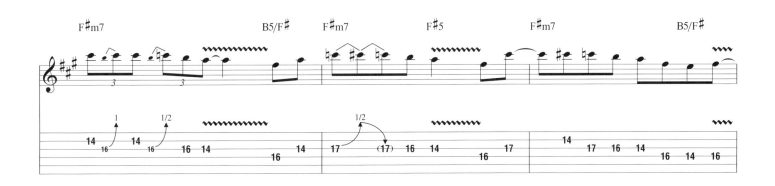

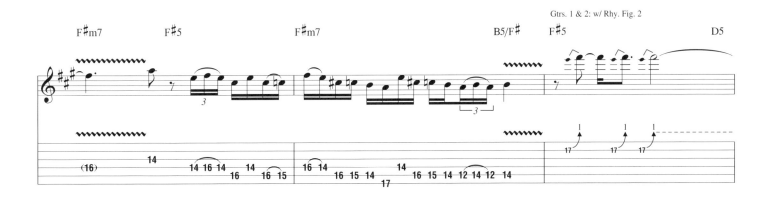

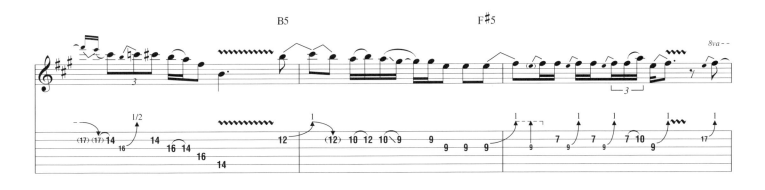

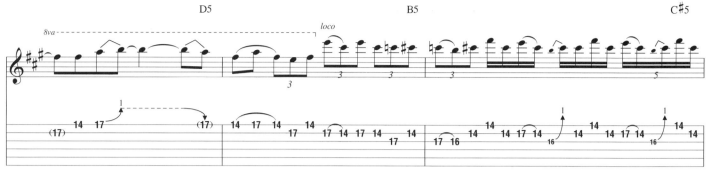

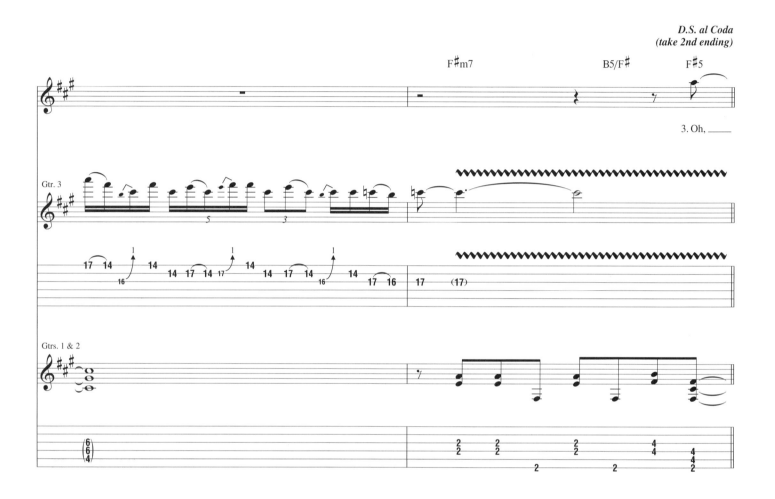

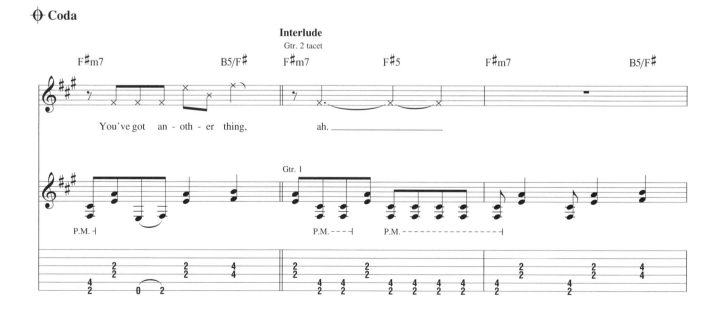

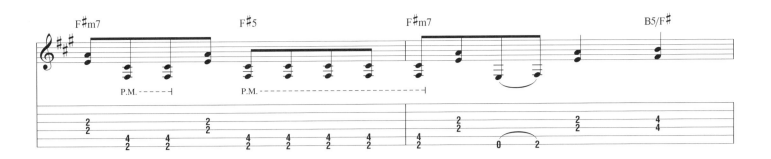

Com - in' on down!

Outro
w/ Voc. ad lib. (till fade)

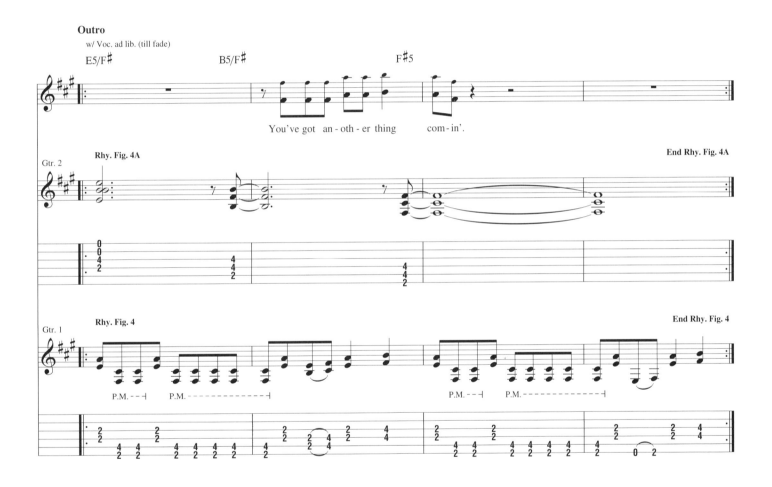

You've got an - oth - er thing com - in'.

Play 8 times & fade

You've got an - oth - er thing com - in'.

(Oh, _____ yeah.) __

Youth Gone Wild

Words and Music by Rachael Bolan Southworth and David Michael Sabo

*Gtr. 1: Dave "The Snake" Sabo; Gtr. 2: Scotti Hill. Composite arrangement

**Decrease to 1/2 vol. w/ vol. knob.

Verse

1. Since I was born, they could-n't hold me down. An-oth-er mis-fit kid, an-
2. A boss scream-in' in my ear a-bout who I'm s'posed to be. Get a three-piece Wall Street smile and,

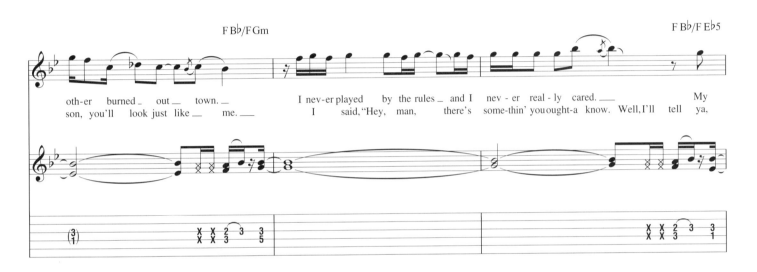

oth-er burned out town. I nev-er played by the rules and I nev-er real-ly cared. My
son, you'll look just like me. I said, "Hey, man, there's some-thin' you ought-a know. Well, I'll tell ya,

2nd time, Gtrs. 1 & 2: w/ Rhy. Fill 2

nas-ty rep-u-ta-tion takes me ev-'ry-where.
Park Av-e-nue leads to skid row."

*Increase to full vol. w/ vol. knob.

Rhy. Fill 2
Gtrs. 1 & 2

**Increase to full vol. w/ vol. knob.

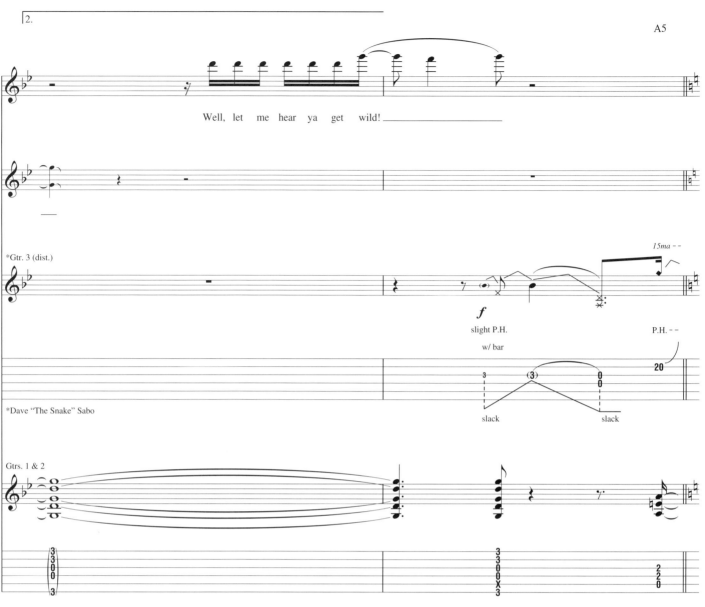

Well, let me hear ya get wild! _____

*Gtr. 3 (dist.)

*Dave "The Snake" Sabo

Gtrs. 1 & 2

Guitar Solo

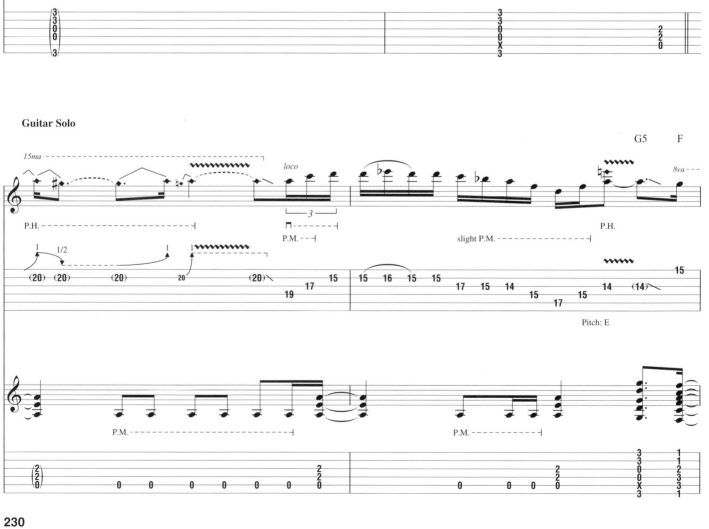

Breakdown

They call us prob-lem _ child. _ We spend our lives on _ trial. _ We walk an end-less _ mile.

_ We stand and we won't _ fall. _

(We are the youth gone _ wild. _

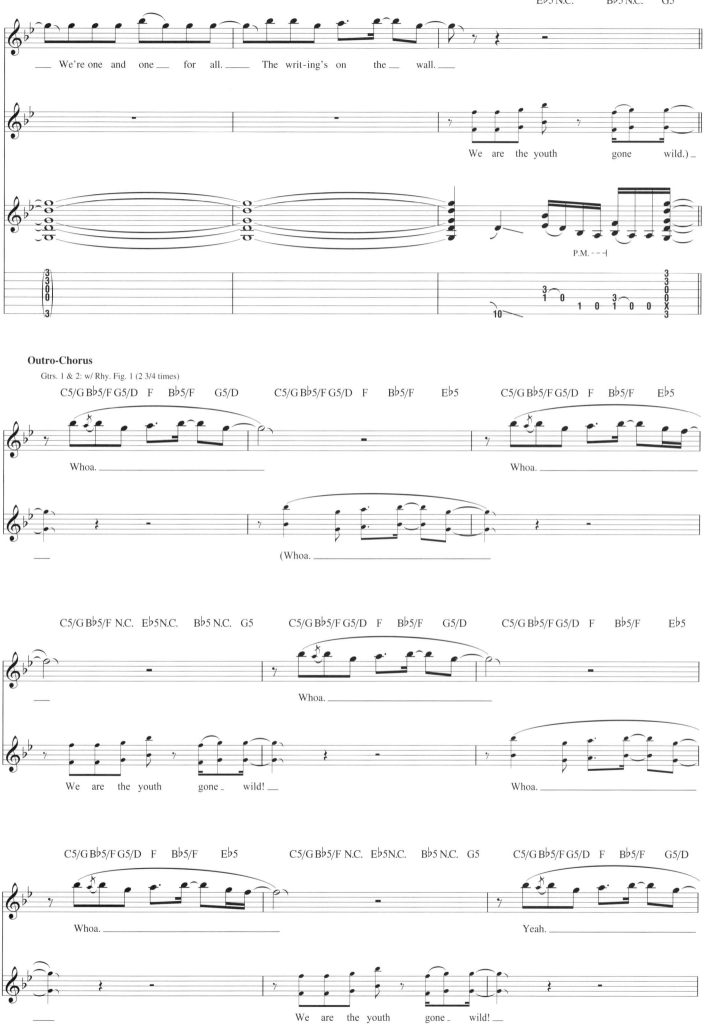

Outro-Chorus

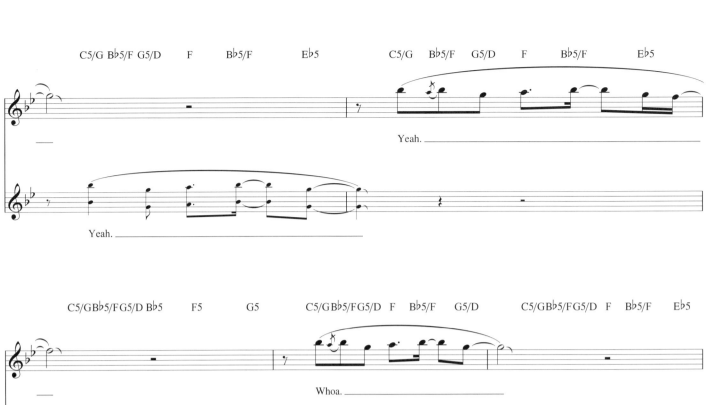

from Scorpions - *Animal Magnetism*

The Zoo

Words and Music by Rudolf Schenker and Klaus Meine

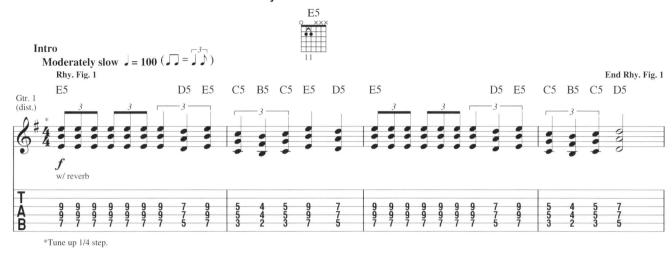

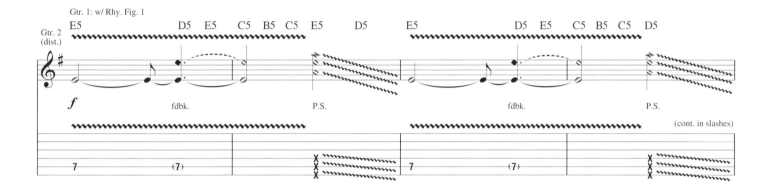

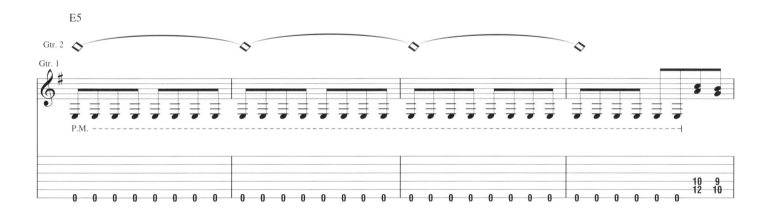

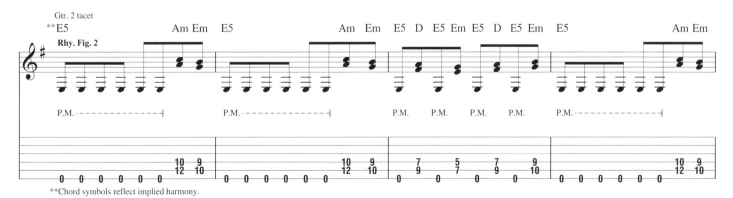

**Chord symbols reflect implied harmony.

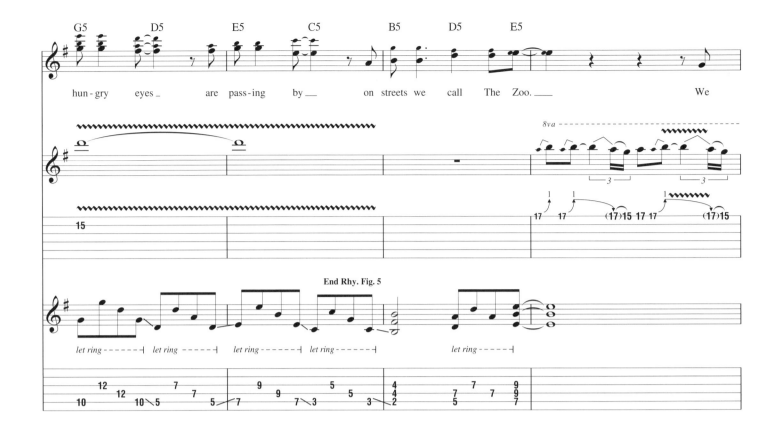

hun - gry eyes _ are pass-ing by _ on streets we call The Zoo. _ We

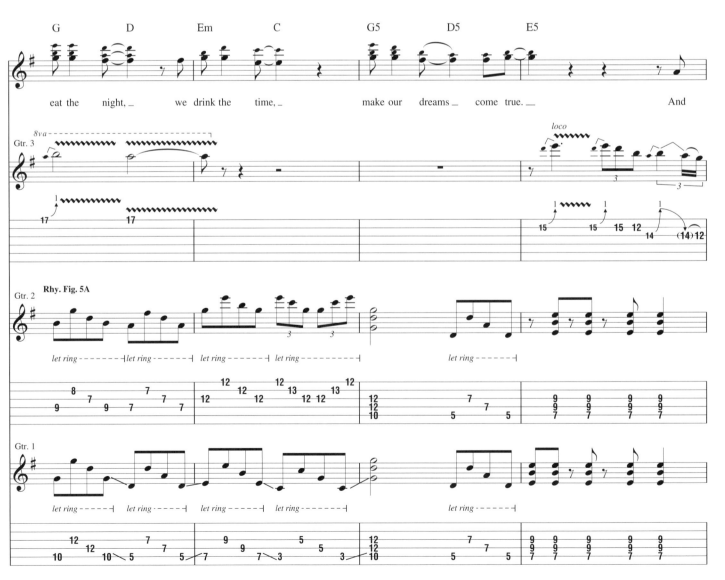

eat the night, _ we drink the time, _ make our dreams _ come true. _ And

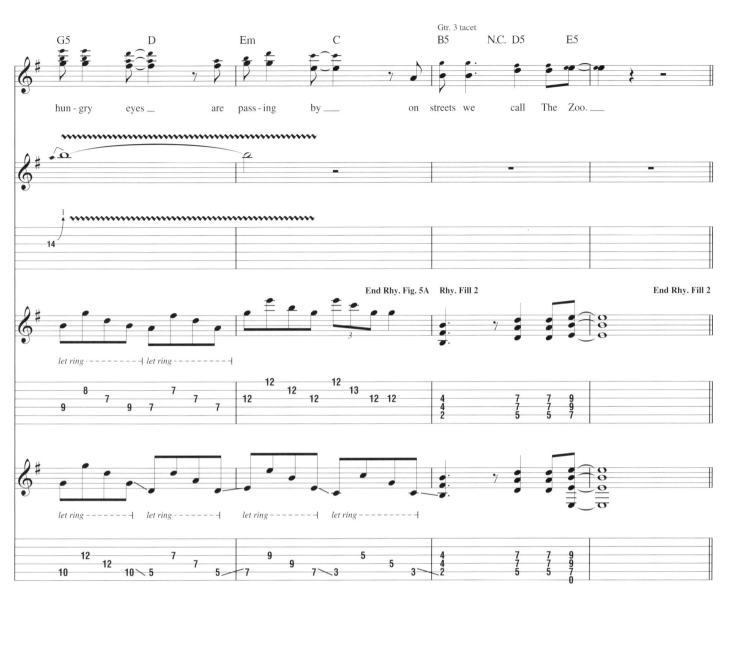

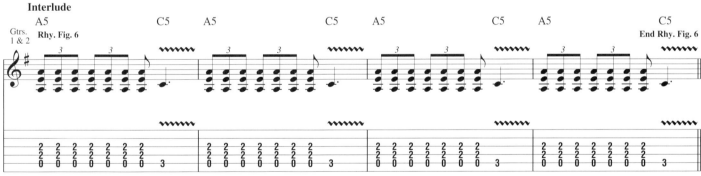

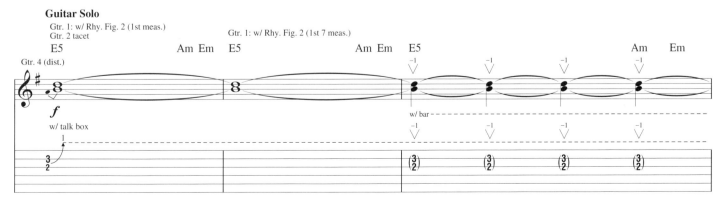

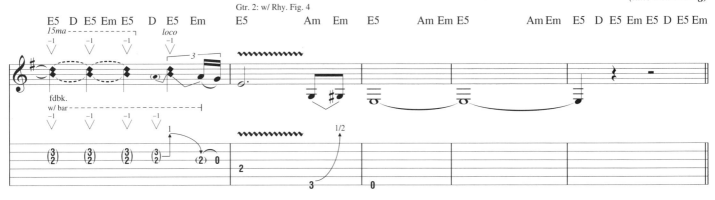

⊕ Coda

Chorus

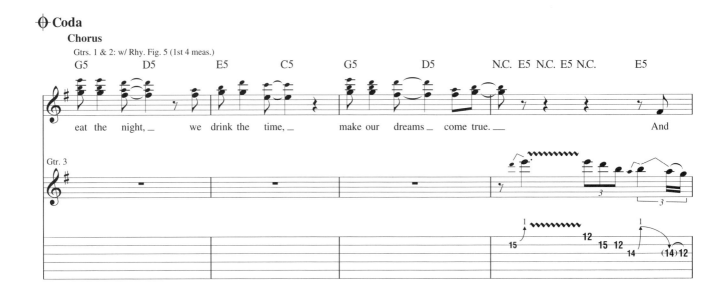

eat the night, ___ we drink the time, ___ make our dreams ___ come true. ___ And

hun-gry eyes ___ are pass-ing by ___ on streets we call The Zoo. ___ We

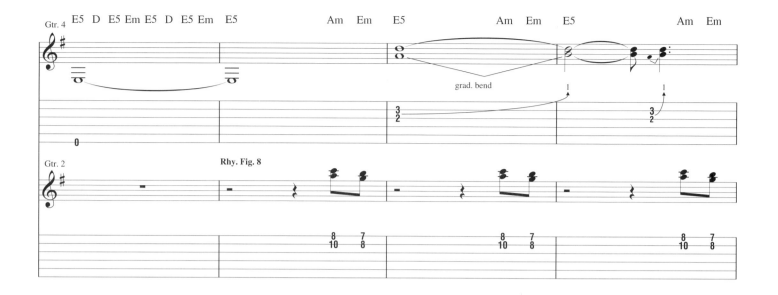

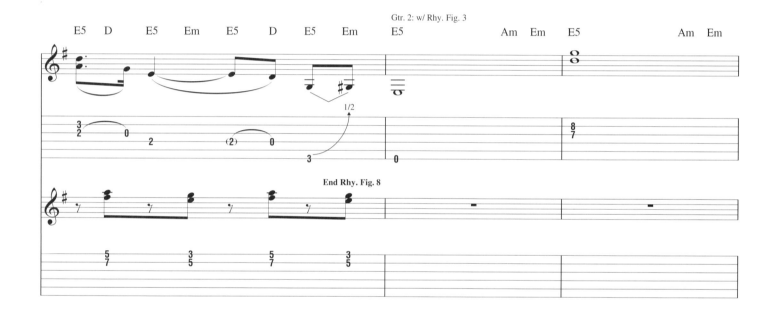

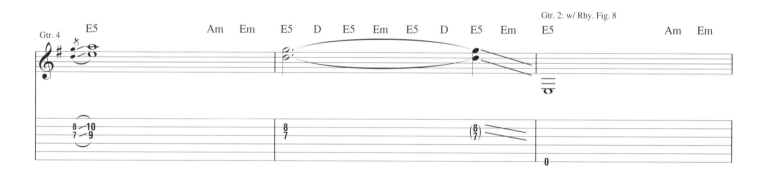

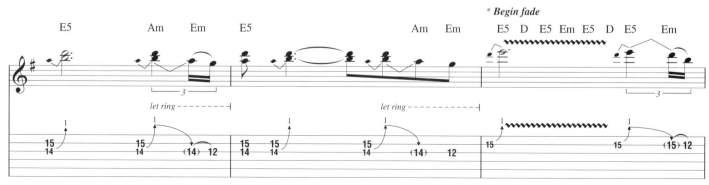

Begin fade

* City soundscape fades in while band fades out.

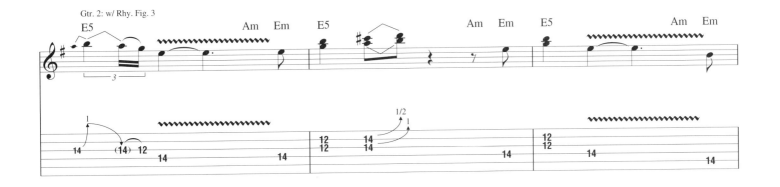

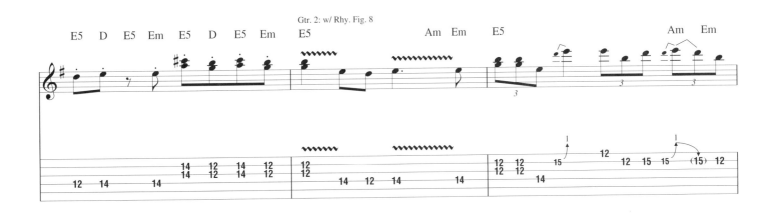

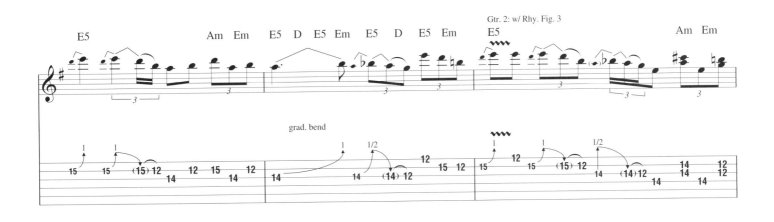

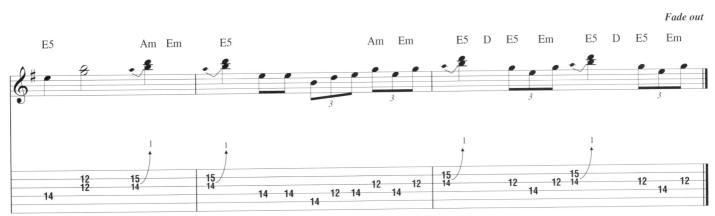

GUITAR NOTATION LEGEND

Guitar music can be notated three different ways: on a *musical staff*, in *tablature*, and in *rhythm slashes*.

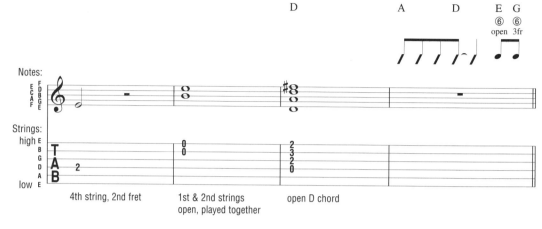

RHYTHM SLASHES are written above the staff. Strum chords in the rhythm indicated. Use the chord diagrams found at the top of the first page of the transcription for the appropriate chord voicings. Round noteheads indicate single notes.

THE MUSICAL STAFF shows pitches and rhythms and is divided by bar lines into measures. Pitches are named after the first seven letters of the alphabet.

TABLATURE graphically represents the guitar fingerboard. Each horizontal line represents a string, and each number represents a fret.

4th string, 2nd fret | 1st & 2nd strings open, played together | open D chord

Definitions for Special Guitar Notation

HALF-STEP BEND: Strike the note and bend up 1/2 step.

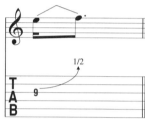

WHOLE-STEP BEND: Strike the note and bend up one step.

GRACE NOTE BEND: Strike the note and immediately bend up as indicated.

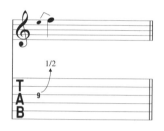

SLIGHT (MICROTONE) BEND: Strike the note and bend up 1/4 step.

BEND AND RELEASE: Strike the note and bend up as indicated, then release back to the original note. Only the first note is struck.

PRE-BEND: Bend the note as indicated, then strike it.

PRE-BEND AND RELEASE: Bend the note as indicated. Strike it and release the bend back to the original note.

UNISON BEND: Strike the two notes simultaneously and bend the lower note up to the pitch of the higher.

VIBRATO: The string is vibrated by rapidly bending and releasing the note with the fretting hand.

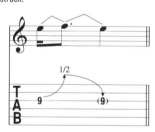

WIDE VIBRATO: The pitch is varied to a greater degree by vibrating with the fretting hand.

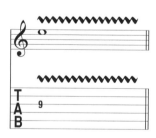

HAMMER-ON: Strike the first (lower) note with one finger, then sound the higher note (on the same string) with another finger by fretting it without picking.

PULL-OFF: Place both fingers on the notes to be sounded. Strike the first note and without picking, pull the finger off to sound the second (lower) note.

LEGATO SLIDE: Strike the first note and then slide the same fret-hand finger up or down to the second note. The second note is not struck.

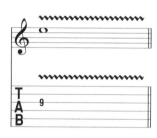

SHIFT SLIDE: Same as legato slide, except the second note is struck.

TRILL: Very rapidly alternate between the notes indicated by continuously hammering on and pulling off.

TAPPING: Hammer ("tap") the fret indicated with the pick-hand index or middle finger and pull off to the note fretted by the fret hand.

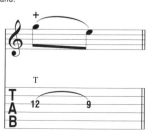

NATURAL HARMONIC: Strike the note while the fret-hand lightly touches the string directly over the fret indicated.

PINCH HARMONIC: The note is fretted normally and a harmonic is produced by adding the edge of the thumb or the tip of the index finger of the pick hand to the normal pick attack.

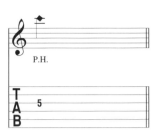

HARP HARMONIC: The note is fretted normally and a harmonic is produced by gently resting the pick hand's index finger directly above the indicated fret (in parentheses) while the pick hand's thumb or pick assists by plucking the appropriate string.

PICK SCRAPE: The edge of the pick is rubbed down (or up) the string, producing a scratchy sound.

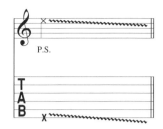

MUFFLED STRINGS: A percussive sound is produced by laying the fret hand across the string(s) without depressing, and striking them with the pick hand.

PALM MUTING: The note is partially muted by the pick hand lightly touching the string(s) just before the bridge.

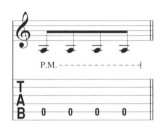

RAKE: Drag the pick across the strings indicated with a single motion.

TREMOLO PICKING: The note is picked as rapidly and continuously as possible.

ARPEGGIATE: Play the notes of the chord indicated by quickly rolling them from bottom to top.

VIBRATO BAR DIVE AND RETURN: The pitch of the note or chord is dropped a specified number of steps (in rhythm), then returned to the original pitch.

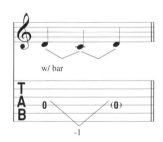

VIBRATO BAR SCOOP: Depress the bar just before striking the note, then quickly release the bar.

VIBRATO BAR DIP: Strike the note and then immediately drop a specified number of steps, then release back to the original pitch.

Additional Musical Definitions

(accent)	•	Accentuate note (play it louder).
(accent)	•	Accentuate note with great intensity.
(staccato)	•	Play the note short.
	•	Downstroke
V	•	Upstroke

D.S. al Coda • Go back to the sign (%), then play until the measure marked "*To Coda*," then skip to the section labelled "**Coda**."

D.C. al Fine • Go back to the beginning of the song and play until the measure marked "*Fine*" (end).

Rhy. Fig. • Label used to recall a recurring accompaniment pattern (usually chordal).

Riff • Label used to recall composed, melodic lines (usually single notes) which recur.

Fill • Label used to identify a brief melodic figure which is to be inserted into the arrangement.

Rhy. Fill • A chordal version of a Fill.

tacet • Instrument is silent (drops out).

• Repeat measures between signs.

• When a repeated section has different endings, play the first ending only the first time and the second ending only the second time.

NOTE: Tablature numbers in parentheses mean:
1. The note is being sustained over a system (note in standard notation is tied), or
2. The note is sustained, but a new articulation (such as a hammer-on, pull-off, slide or vibrato) begins, or
3. The note is a barely audible "ghost" note (note in standard notation is also in parentheses).

GUITAR RECORDED VERSIONS®

AUTHENTIC TRANSCRIPTIONS WITH NOTES AND TABLATURE

Guitar Recorded Versions® are note-for-note transcriptions of guitar music taken directly off recordings
This series, one of the most popular in print today, features some of the greatest guitar players and groups from blues and rock to country and jazz.

Guitar Recorded Versions are transcribed by the best transcribers in the business
*Every book contains notes and tablature. Visit **www.halleonard.com** for our complete selection.*

14041344	The Definitive AC/DC Songbook	$39.99
00690016	The Will Ackerman Collection	$19.95
00690501	Bryan Adams – Greatest Hits	$19.95
00690002	Aerosmith – Big Ones	$24.95
00692015	Aerosmith – Greatest Hits	$22.95
00690603	Aerosmith – O Yeah! (Ultimate Hits)	$24.95
00690147	Aerosmith – Rocks	$19.95
00690146	Aerosmith – Toys in the Attic	$19.99
00690178	Alice in Chains – Acoustic	$19.95
00694865	Alice in Chains – Dirt	$19.95
00660225	Alice in Chains – Facelift	$19.95
00694925	Alice in Chains – Jar of Flies/Sap	$19.95
00690387	Alice in Chains – Nothing Safe: Best of the Box	$19.95
00690899	All That Remains – The Fall of Ideals	$22.99
00691056	All That Remains – For We Are Many	$22.99
00690980	All That Remains – Overcome	$22.99
00690812	All-American Rejects – Move Along	$19.95
00690983	All-American Rejects – When the World Comes Down	$22.99
00694932	Allman Brothers Band – Definitive Collection for Guitar Volume 1	$24.95
00694933	Allman Brothers Band – Definitive Collection for Guitar Volume 2	$24.95
00694934	Allman Brothers Band – Definitive Collection for Guitar Volume 3	$24.95
00690958	Duane Allman Guitar Anthology	$24.99
00691071	Alter Bridge – AB III	$22.99
00690945	Alter Bridge – Blackbird	$22.99
00690755	Alter Bridge – One Day Remains	$22.99
00690571	Trey Anastasio	$19.95
00691013	The Answer – Everyday Demons	$19.99
00690158	Chet Atkins – Almost Alone	$19.95
00694876	Chet Atkins – Contemporary Styles	$19.95
00694878	Chet Atkins – Vintage Fingerstyle	$19.95
00690865	Atreyu – A Deathgrip on Yesterday	$19.95
00690609	Audioslave	$19.95
00690804	Audioslave – Out of Exile	$19.95
00690884	Audioslave – Revelations	$19.95
00690926	Avenged Sevenfold	$22.95
00690820	Avenged Sevenfold – City of Evil	$24.95
00691065	Avenged Sevenfold – Waking the Fallen	$22.99
00694918	Randy Bachman Collection	$22.95
00690503	Beach Boys – Very Best of	$19.95
00694929	Beatles: 1962-1966	$24.99
00694930	Beatles: 1967-1970	$24.95
00690489	Beatles – 1	$24.99
00694880	Beatles – Abbey Road	$19.95
00691066	Beatles – Beatles for Sale	$22.99
00690110	Beatles – Book 1 (White Album)	$19.95
00690111	Beatles – Book 2 (White Album)	$19.95
00690902	Beatles – The Capitol Albums, Volume 1	$24.99
00694832	Beatles – For Acoustic Guitar	$22.99
00690137	Beatles – A Hard Day's Night	$16.95
00691031	Beatles – Help!	$19.99
00690482	Beatles – Let It Be	$17.95
00691067	Beatles – Meet the Beatles!	$22.99
00691068	Beatles – Please Please Me	$22.99
00694891	Beatles – Revolver	$19.95
00694914	Beatles – Rubber Soul	$22.99
00694863	Beatles – Sgt. Pepper's Lonely Hearts Club Band	$22.99
00110193	Beatles – Tomorrow Never Knows	$22.99
00690383	Beatles – Yellow Submarine	$19.95
00691044	Jeff Beck – Best of Beck	$24.99
00690632	Beck – Sea Change	$19.95
00691041	Jeff Beck – Truth	$19.99
00694884	Best of George Benson	$19.95
00692385	Chuck Berry	$19.95
00690835	Billy Talent	$19.95
00690879	Billy Talent II	$19.95
00690149	Black Sabbath	$16.99
00690901	Best of Black Sabbath	$19.95
00691010	Black Sabbath – Heaven and Hell	$22.99
00690148	Black Sabbath – Master of Reality	$16.99
00690142	Black Sabbath – Paranoid	$16.99
00692200	Black Sabbath – We Sold Our Soul for Rock 'N' Roll	$19.95
00690389	blink-182 – Enema of the State	$19.95
00690831	blink-182 – Greatest Hits	$19.95
00691179	blink-182 – Neighborhoods	$22.99
00690523	blink-182 – Take Off Your Pants and Jacket	$19.95
00690028	Blue Oyster Cult – Cult Classics	$19.95
00690008	Bon Jovi – Cross Road	$19.95
00691074	Bon Jovi – Greatest Hits	$22.99
00690913	Boston	$19.95
00690932	Boston – Don't Look Back	$19.99
00690829	Boston Guitar Collection	$19.99
00690491	Best of David Bowie	$19.95
00690583	Box Car Racer	$19.95
00691023	Breaking Benjamin – Dear Agony	$22.99
00690873	Breaking Benjamin – Phobia	$19.95
00690764	Breaking Benjamin – We Are Not Alone	$19.95
00690451	Jeff Buckley Collection	$24.95
00690957	Bullet for My Valentine – Scream Aim Fire	$22.99
00690678	Best of Kenny Burrell	$19.95
00691077	Cage the Elephant – Thank You, Happy Birthday	$22.99
00690564	The Calling – Camino Palmero	$19.95
00691159	The Cars – Complete Greatest Hits	$22.99
00690261	Carter Family Collection	$19.95
00691079	Best of Johnny Cash	$22.99
00690043	Best of Cheap Trick	$19.95
00690171	Chicago – The Definitive Guitar Collection	$22.95
00691004	Chickenfoot	$22.99
00691011	Chimaira Guitar Collection	$24.99
00690567	Charlie Christian – The Definitive Collection	$19.95
00101916	Eric Church – Chief	$22.99
00690590	Eric Clapton – Anthology	$29.95
00692391	Best of Eric Clapton – 2nd Edition	$22.95
00691055	Eric Clapton – Clapton	$22.99
00690936	Eric Clapton – Complete Clapton	$29.99
00690074	Eric Clapton – Cream of Clapton	$24.95
00690247	Eric Clapton – 461 Ocean Boulevard	$19.99
00690010	Eric Clapton – From the Cradle	$19.95
00690363	Eric Clapton – Just One Night	$24.99
00694873	Eric Clapton – Timepieces	$19.95
00694869	Eric Clapton – Unplugged	$22.95
00690415	Clapton Chronicles – Best of Eric Clapton	$18.95
00694896	John Mayall/Eric Clapton – Bluesbreakers	$19.95
00690162	Best of the Clash	$19.95
00690828	Coheed & Cambria – Good Apollo I'm Burning Star, IV, Vol. 1: From Fear Through the Eyes of Madness	$19.95
00690940	Coheed and Cambria – No World for Tomorrow	$19.95
00690494	Coldplay – Parachutes	$19.95
00690593	Coldplay – A Rush of Blood to the Head	$19.95
00690806	Coldplay – X & Y	$19.95
00690855	Best of Collective Soul	$19.95
00691091	The Best of Alice Cooper	$22.99
00694940	Counting Crows – August & Everything After	$19.95
00690405	Counting Crows – This Desert Life	$19.95
00694840	Cream – Disraeli Gears	$19.95
00690285	Cream – Those Were the Days	$17.95
00690819	Best of Creedence Clearwater Revival	$22.95
00690648	The Very Best of Jim Croce	$19.95
00690572	Steve Cropper – Soul Man	$19.95
00690613	Best of Crosby, Stills & Nash	$22.95
00690777	Crossfade	$19.95
00699521	The Cure – Greatest Hits	$24.95
00690637	Best of Dick Dale	$19.95
00690892	Daughtry	$19.95
00690822	Best of Alex De Grassi	$19.95
00690967	Death Cab for Cutie – Narrow Stairs	$22.99
00690289	Best of Deep Purple	$19.99
00690288	Deep Purple – Machine Head	$17.99
00690784	Best of Def Leppard	$19.95
00694831	Derek and the Dominos – Layla & Other Assorted Love Songs	$22.95
00692240	Bo Diddley – Guitar Solos by Fred Sokolow	$19.99
00690384	Best of Ani DiFranco	$19.95
00690322	Ani DiFranco – Little Plastic Castle	$19.95
00690380	Ani DiFranco – Up Up Up Up Up Up	$19.95
00690979	Best of Dinosaur Jr.	$19.99
00690833	Private Investigations – Best of Dire Straits and Mark Knopfler	$24.95
00695382	Very Best of Dire Straits – Sultans of Swing	$22.95
00690347	The Doors – Anthology	$22.95
00690348	The Doors – Essential Guitar Collection	$16.95
00690915	Dragonforce – Inhuman Rampage	$29.99
00690250	Best of Duane Eddy	$16.95
00690533	Electric Light Orchestra Guitar Collection	$19.95
00690909	Best of Tommy Emmanuel	$22.99
00690555	Best of Melissa Etheridge	$19.95
00690515	Extreme II – Pornograffitti	$19.95
00690982	Fall Out Boy – Folie à Deux	$22.99
00690810	Fall Out Boy – From Under the Cork Tree	$19.95
00691009	Five Finger Death Punch	$19.99
00690664	Best of Fleetwood Mac	$19.95
00690870	Flyleaf	$19.95
00690257	John Fogerty – Blue Moon Swamp	$19.95
00690931	Foo Fighters – Echoes, Silence, Patience & Grace	$19.95
00690808	Foo Fighters – In Your Honor	$19.95
00691115	Foo Fighters – Wasting Light	$22.99
00690805	Best of Robben Ford	$22.99
00690842	Best of Peter Frampton	$19.95
00690734	Franz Ferdinand	$19.95
00694920	Best of Free	$19.95
00694807	Danny Gatton – 88 Elmira St	$19.95
00690438	Genesis Guitar Anthology	$19.95
00690753	Best of Godsmack	$19.95
00120167	Godsmack	$19.95
00690338	Goo Goo Dolls – Dizzy Up the Girl	$19.95
00113073	Green Day – Uno	$21.99
00690927	Patty Griffin – Children Running Through	$19.95
00690591	Patty Griffin – Guitar Collection	$19.95
00690978	Guns N' Roses – Chinese Democracy	$24.99
00691027	Buddy Guy Anthology	$24.99
00694854	Buddy Guy – Damn Right, I've Got the Blues	$19.95
00690697	Best of Jim Hall	$19.95
00690840	Ben Harper – Both Sides of the Gun	$19.95
00691018	Ben Harper – Fight for Your Mind	$22.99
00690987	Ben Harper and Relentless7 – White Lies for Dark Times	$22.99
00694798	George Harrison Anthology	$19.95
00690778	Hawk Nelson – Letters to the President	$19.95
00690841	Scott Henderson – Blues Guitar Collection	$19.95
00692930	Jimi Hendrix – Are You Experienced?	$24.95
00692931	Jimi Hendrix – Axis: Bold As Love	$22.95
00690304	Jimi Hendrix – Band of Gypsys	$24.99
00690608	Jimi Hendrix – Blue Wild Angel	$24.95
00694944	Jimi Hendrix – Blues	$24.95
00692932	Jimi Hendrix – Electric Ladyland	$24.95
00690602	Jimi Hendrix – Smash Hits	$24.99
00691033	Jimi Hendrix – Valleys of Neptune	$22.99
00691152	West Coast Seattle Boy: The Jimi Hendrix Anthology	$29.99
00691332	Jimi Hendrix – Winterland (Highlights)	$22.99
00690017	Jimi Hendrix – Woodstock	$24.95
00690843	H.I.M. – Dark Light	$19.95
00690869	Hinder – Extreme Behavior	$19.95
00660029	Buddy Holly	$22.99
00690793	John Lee Hooker Anthology	$24.99
00660169	John Lee Hooker – A Blues Legend	$19.95
00694905	Howlin' Wolf	$19.95
00690692	Very Best of Billy Idol	$19.95
00690688	Incubus – A Crow Left of the Murder	$19.95
00690136	Indigo Girls – 1200 Curfews	$22.95
00690790	Iron Maiden Anthology	$24.99
00691058	Iron Maiden – The Final Frontier	$22.99
00690887	Iron Maiden – A Matter of Life and Death	$24.95
00690730	Alan Jackson – Guitar Collection	$19.95
00694938	Elmore James – Master Electric Slide Guitar	$19.95
00690652	Best of Jane's Addiction	$19.95
00690721	Jet – Get Born	$19.95
00690684	Jethro Tull – Aqualung	$19.95
00690693	Jethro Tull Guitar Anthology	$19.95
00691182	Jethro Tull – Stand Up	$22.99
00690647	Best of Jewel	$19.95

00690898	John 5 – The Devil Knows My Name	$22.95
00690959	John 5 – Requiem	$22.95
00690814	John 5 – Songs for Sanity	$19.95
00690751	John 5 – Vertigo	$19.95
00694912	Eric Johnson – Ah Via Musicom	$19.95
00690660	Best of Eric Johnson	$22.99
00690845	Eric Johnson – Bloom	$19.95
00691076	Eric Johnson – Up Close	$22.99
00690169	Eric Johnson – Venus Isle	$22.95
00690846	Jack Johnson and Friends – Sing-A-Longs and Lullabies for the Film Curious George	$19.95
00690271	Robert Johnson – The New Transcriptions	$24.95
00699131	Best of Janis Joplin	$19.95
00690427	Best of Judas Priest	$22.99
00690651	Juanes – Exitos de Juanes	$19.95
00690277	Best of Kansas	$19.95
00690911	Best of Phil Keaggy	$24.99
00690727	Toby Keith Guitar Collection	$19.99
00690888	The Killers – Sam's Town	$19.95
00690504	Very Best of Albert King	$19.95
00690444	B.B. King & Eric Clapton – Riding with the King	$22.99
00690134	Freddie King Collection	$19.95
00691062	Kings of Leon – Come Around Sundown	$22.99
00690975	Kings of Leon – Only by the Night	$22.99
00690339	Best of the Kinks	$19.95
00690157	Kiss – Alive!	$19.95
00690356	Kiss – Alive II	$22.99
00694903	Best of Kiss for Guitar	$24.95
00690355	Kiss – Destroyer	$16.95
14026320	Mark Knopfler – Get Lucky	$22.99
00690164	Mark Knopfler Guitar – Vol. 1	$19.95
00690163	Mark Knopfler/Chet Atkins – Neck and Neck	$19.95
00690780	Korn – Greatest Hits, Volume 1	$22.95
00690836	Korn – See You on the Other Side	$19.95
00690377	Kris Kristofferson Collection	$19.95
00690861	Kutless – Hearts of the Innocent	$19.95
00690834	Lamb of God – Ashes of the Wake	$19.95
00690875	Lamb of God – Sacrament	$19.95
00690977	Ray LaMontagne – Gossip in the Grain	$19.99
00690890	Ray LaMontagne – Till the Sun Turns Black	$19.95
00690823	Ray LaMontagne – Trouble	$19.95
00691057	Ray LaMontagne and the Pariah Dogs – God Willin' & The Creek Don't Rise	$22.99
00690658	Johnny Lang – Long Time Coming	$19.95
00690679	John Lennon – Guitar Collection	$19.95
00690781	Linkin Park – Hybrid Theory	$22.95
00690782	Linkin Park – Meteora	$22.95
00690922	Linkin Park – Minutes to Midnight	$19.95
00690783	Best of Live	$19.95
00699623	The Best of Chuck Loeb	$19.95
00690743	Los Lonely Boys	$19.95
00690720	Lostprophets – Start Something	$19.95
00690525	Best of George Lynch	$24.99
00690955	Lynyrd Skynyrd – All-Time Greatest Hits	$19.99
00694954	New Best of Lynyrd Skynyrd	$19.95
00690577	Yngwie Malmsteen – Anthology	$24.95
00694845	Yngwie Malmsteen – Fire and Ice	$19.95
00694757	Yngwie Malmsteen – Trilogy	$19.95
00690754	Marilyn Manson – Lest We Forget	$19.95
00694956	Bob Marley – Legend	$19.95
00690548	Very Best of Bob Marley & The Wailers – One Love	$22.99
00694945	Bob Marley – Songs of Freedom	$24.95
00690914	Maroon 5 – It Won't Be Soon Before Long	$19.95
00690657	Maroon 5 – Songs About Jane	$19.95
00690748	Maroon 5 – 1.22.03 Acoustic	$19.95
00690989	Mastodon – Crack the Skye	$22.99
00691176	Mastodon – The Hunter	$22.99
00690442	Matchbox 20 – Mad Season	$19.95
00690616	Matchbox Twenty – More Than You Think You Are	$19.95
00690239	Matchbox 20 – Yourself or Someone like You	$19.95
00691034	Andy McKee – Joyland	$19.99
00690382	Sarah McLachlan – Mirrorball	$19.95
00120080	The Don McLean Songbook	$19.95
00694952	Megadeth – Countdown to Extinction	$22.95
00690244	Megadeth – Cryptic Writings	$19.95
00694951	Megadeth – Rust in Peace	$22.95
00690011	Megadeth – Youthanasia	$19.95
00690505	John Mellencamp Guitar Collection	$19.95
00690562	Pat Metheny – Bright Size Life	$19.95
00691073	Pat Metheny with Christian McBride & Antonion Sanchez – Day Trip/Tokyo Day Trip Live	$22.99
00690646	Pat Metheny – One Quiet Night	$19.95
00690559	Pat Metheny – Question & Answer	$19.95
00690040	Steve Miller Band Greatest Hits	$19.95
00690769	Modest Mouse – Good News for People Who Love Bad News	$19.95
00102591	Wes Montgomery Guitar Anthology	$24.99
00694802	Gary Moore – Still Got the Blues	$22.99
00691005	Best of Motion City Soundtrack	$19.99
00690787	Mudvayne – L.D. 50	$22.95
00691070	Mumford & Sons – Sigh No More	$22.99
00690996	My Morning Jacket Collection	$19.99
00690984	Matt Nathanson – Some Mad Hope	$22.99
00690611	Nirvana	$22.95
00694895	Nirvana – Bleach	$19.95
00690189	Nirvana – From the Muddy Banks of the Wishkah	$19.95
00694913	Nirvana – In Utero	$19.95
00694883	Nirvana – Nevermind	$19.95
00690026	Nirvana – Unplugged in New York	$19.95
00120112	No Doubt – Tragic Kingdom	$22.95
00690226	Oasis – The Other Side of Oasis	$19.95
00307163	Oasis – Time Flies... 1994-2009	$19.99
00690358	The Offspring – Americana	$19.95
00690203	The Offspring – Smash	$18.95
00690818	The Best of Opeth	$22.95
00691052	Roy Orbison – Black & White Night	$22.99
00694847	Best of Ozzy Osbourne	$22.95
00690399	Ozzy Osbourne – The Ozzman Cometh	$22.99
00690129	Ozzy Osbourne – Ozzmosis	$22.95
00690933	Best of Brad Paisley	$22.95
00690995	Brad Paisley – Play: The Guitar Album	$24.99
00690866	Panic! At the Disco – A Fever You Can't Sweat Out	$19.95
00690939	Christopher Parkening – Solo Pieces	$19.99
00690594	Best of Les Paul	$19.95
00694855	Pearl Jam – Ten	$22.99
00690439	A Perfect Circle – Mer De Noms	$19.95
00690661	A Perfect Circle – Thirteenth Step	$19.95
00690725	Best of Carl Perkins	$19.99
00690499	Tom Petty – Definitive Guitar Collection	$19.95
00690868	Tom Petty – Highway Companion	$19.95
00690176	Phish – Billy Breathes	$22.95
00691249	Phish – Junta	$22.99
00690428	Pink Floyd – Dark Side of the Moon	$19.95
00690789	Best of Poison	$19.95
00693864	Best of The Police	$19.95
00690299	Best of Elvis: The King of Rock 'n' Roll	$19.95
00692535	Elvis Presley	$19.95
00690925	The Very Best of Prince	$22.99
00690003	Classic Queen	$24.95
00694975	Queen – Greatest Hits	$24.95
00690670	Very Best of Queensryche	$19.95
00690878	The Raconteurs – Broken Boy Soldiers	$19.95
00694910	Rage Against the Machine	$19.95
00690179	Rancid – And Out Come the Wolves	$22.95
00690426	Best of Ratt	$19.95
00690055	Red Hot Chili Peppers – Blood Sugar Sex Magik	$19.95
00690584	Red Hot Chili Peppers – By the Way	$19.95
00690379	Red Hot Chili Peppers – Californication	$19.95
00690673	Red Hot Chili Peppers – Greatest Hits	$19.95
00690090	Red Hot Chili Peppers – One Hot Minute	$22.95
00691166	Red Hot Chili Peppers – I'm with You	$22.99
00690852	Red Hot Chili Peppers – Stadium Arcadium	$24.95
00690893	The Red Jumpsuit Apparatus – Don't You Fake It	$19.95
00690511	Django Reinhardt – The Definitive Collection	$19.95
00690779	Relient K – MMHMM	$19.95
00690643	Relient K – Two Lefts Don't Make a Right ... But Three Do	$19.95
00690260	Jimmie Rodgers Guitar Collection	$19.95
14041901	Rodrigo Y Gabriela and C.U.B.A. – Area 52	$24.99
00690014	Rolling Stones – Exile on Main Street	$24.95
00690631	Rolling Stones – Guitar Anthology	$27.95
00690685	David Lee Roth – Eat 'Em and Smile	$19.95
00690031	Santana's Greatest Hits	$19.95
00690796	Very Best of Michael Schenker	$19.95
00690566	Best of Scorpions	$22.95
00690604	Bob Seger – Guitar Anthology	$19.95
00690659	Bob Seger and the Silver Bullet Band – Greatest Hits, Volume 2	$17.95
00691012	Shadows Fall – Retribution	$22.99
00690896	Shadows Fall – Threads of Life	$19.95
00690803	Best of Kenny Wayne Shepherd Band	$19.95
00690750	Kenny Wayne Shepherd – The Place You're In	$19.95
00690857	Shinedown – Us and Them	$19.95
00690196	Silverchair – Freak Show	$19.95
00690130	Silverchair – Frogstomp	$19.95
00690872	Slayer – Christ Illusion	$19.95
00690813	Slayer – Guitar Collection	$19.95
00690419	Slipknot	$19.95
00690973	Slipknot – All Hope Is Gone	$22.99
00690733	Slipknot – Volume 3 (The Subliminal Verses)	$22.99
00690330	Social Distortion – Live at the Roxy	$19.95
00120004	Best of Steely Dan	$24.95
00694921	Best of Steppenwolf	$22.95
00690655	Best of Mike Stern	$19.95
00690949	Rod Stewart Guitar Anthology	$19.99
00690021	Sting – Fields of Gold	$19.95
00690689	Story of the Year – Page Avenue	$19.95
00690520	Styx Guitar Collection	$19.95
00120081	Sublime	$19.95
00690992	Sublime – Robbin' the Hood	$19.99
00690519	SUM 41 – All Killer No Filler	$19.95
00691072	Best of Supertramp	$22.99
00690994	Taylor Swift	$22.99
00690993	Taylor Swift – Fearless	$22.99
00691063	Taylor Swift – Speak Now	$22.99
00690767	Switchfoot – The Beautiful Letdown	$19.95
00690830	System of a Down – Hypnotize	$19.95
00690531	System of a Down – Toxicity	$19.95
00694824	Best of James Taylor	$16.95
00694887	Best of Thin Lizzy	$19.95
00690871	Three Days Grace – One-X	$19.95
00690891	30 Seconds to Mars – A Beautiful Lie	$19.95
00690030	Toad the Wet Sprocket	$19.95
00690233	The Merle Travis Collection	$19.99
00690683	Robin Trower – Bridge of Sighs	$19.95
00699191	U2 – Best of: 1980-1990	$19.95
00690732	U2 – Best of: 1990-2000	$19.95
00690894	U2 – 18 Singles	$19.95
00690775	U2 – How to Dismantle an Atomic Bomb	$22.95
00690997	U2 – No Line on the Horizon	$19.99
00690039	Steve Vai – Alien Love Secrets	$24.95
00690172	Steve Vai – Fire Garden	$24.95
00660137	Steve Vai – Passion & Warfare	$24.95
00690881	Steve Vai – Real Illusions: Reflections	$24.95
00694904	Steve Vai – Sex and Religion	$24.95
00690392	Steve Vai – The Ultra Zone	$19.95
00690024	Stevie Ray Vaughan – Couldn't Stand the Weather	$19.95
00690370	Stevie Ray Vaughan and Double Trouble – The Real Deal: Greatest Hits Volume 2	$22.95
00690116	Stevie Ray Vaughan – Guitar Collection	$24.95
00660136	Stevie Ray Vaughan – In Step	$19.95
00694879	Stevie Ray Vaughan – In the Beginning	$19.95
00660058	Stevie Ray Vaughan – Lightnin' Blues '83-'87	$24.95
00690036	Stevie Ray Vaughan – Live Alive	$24.95
00694835	Stevie Ray Vaughan – The Sky Is Crying	$22.95
00690025	Stevie Ray Vaughan – Soul to Soul	$19.95
00690015	Stevie Ray Vaughan – Texas Flood	$19.95
00690772	Velvet Revolver – Contraband	$22.95
00690132	The T-Bone Walker Collection	$19.95
00694789	Muddy Waters – Deep Blues	$24.95
00690071	Weezer (The Blue Album)	$19.95
00690516	Weezer (The Green Album)	$19.95
00690286	Weezer – Pinkerton	$19.95
00691046	Weezer – Rarities Edition	$22.99
00690447	Best of the Who	$24.95
00694970	The Who – Definitive Guitar Collection: A-E	$24.95
00694971	The Who – Definitive Guitar Collection F-Li	$24.95
00694972	The Who – Definitive Guitar Collection: Lo-R	$24.95
00690672	Best of Dar Williams	$19.95
00691017	Wolfmother – Cosmic Egg	$22.99
00690319	Stevie Wonder – Some of the Best	$17.95
00690596	Best of the Yardbirds	$19.95
00690844	Yellowcard – Lights and Sounds	$19.95
00690916	The Best of Dwight Yoakam	$19.95
00690904	Neil Young – Harvest	$29.99
00690905	Neil Young – Rust Never Sleeps	$19.99
00690443	Frank Zappa – Hot Rats	$19.95
00690624	Frank Zappa and the Mothers of Invention – One Size Fits All	$22.99
00690623	Frank Zappa – Over-Nite Sensation	$22.99
00690589	ZZ Top – Guitar Anthology	$24.95
00690960	ZZ Top Guitar Classics	$19.99

RECORDED VERSIONS GUITAR®

AUTHENTIC TRANSCRIPTIONS WITH NOTES AND TABLATURE

HAL•LEONARD® CORPORATION

7777 W. Bluemound Rd. P.O. Box 13819 Milwaukee, WI 53213

Complete songlists and more at www.halleonard.com

Prices, contents, and availability subject to change without notice.

1112

Get Better at Guitar

...with these Great Guitar Instruction Books from Hal Leonard!

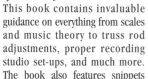

101 GUITAR TIPS
INCLUDES TAB

STUFF ALL THE PROS KNOW AND USE
by Adam St. James
This book contains invaluable guidance on everything from scales and music theory to truss rod adjustments, proper recording studio set-ups, and much more. The book also features snippets of advice from some of the most celebrated guitarists and producers in the music business, including B.B. King, Steve Vai, Joe Satriani, Warren Haynes, Laurence Juber, Pete Anderson, Tom Dowd and others, culled from the author's hundreds of interviews.
00695737 Book/CD Pack.........................$16.95

AMAZING PHRASING
INCLUDES TAB

50 WAYS TO IMPROVE YOUR IMPROVISATIONAL SKILLS
by Tom Kolb
This book/CD pack explores all the main components necessary for crafting well-balanced rhythmic and melodic phrases. It also explains how these phrases are put together to form cohesive solos. Many styles are covered – rock, blues, jazz, fusion, country, Latin, funk and more – and all of the concepts are backed up with musical examples. The companion CD contains 89 demos for listening, and most tracks feature full-band backing.
00695583 Book/CD Pack.........................$19.95

BLUES YOU CAN USE
INCLUDES TAB

by John Ganapes
A comprehensive source designed to help guitarists develop both lead and rhythm playing. Covers: Texas, Delta, R&B, early rock and roll, gospel, blues/rock and more. Includes: 21 complete solos • chord progressions and riffs • turnarounds • moveable scales and more. CD features leads and full band backing.
00695007 Book/CD Pack.........................$19.99

FRETBOARD MASTERY
INCLUDES TAB

by Troy Stetina
Untangle the mysterious regions of the guitar fretboard and unlock your potential. *Fretboard Mastery* familiarizes you with all the shapes you need to know by applying them in real musical examples, thereby reinforcing and reaffirming your newfound knowledge. The result is a much higher level of comprehension and retention.
00695331 Book/CD Pack.........................$19.95

FRETBOARD ROADMAPS – 2ND EDITION

ESSENTIAL GUITAR PATTERNS THAT ALL THE PROS KNOW AND USE
by Fred Sokolow
The updated edition of this bestseller features more songs, updated lessons, and a full audio CD! Learn to play lead and rhythm anywhere on the fretboard, in any key; play a variety of lead guitar styles; play chords and progressions anywhere on the fretboard; expand your chord vocabulary; and learn to think musically – the way the pros do.
00695941 Book/CD Pack.........................$14.95

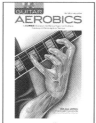

GUITAR AEROBICS
INCLUDES TAB

A 52-WEEK, ONE-LICK-PER-DAY WORKOUT PROGRAM FOR DEVELOPING, IMPROVING & MAINTAINING GUITAR TECHNIQUE
by Troy Nelson
From the former editor of *Guitar One* magazine, here is a daily dose of vitamins to keep your chops fine tuned! Musical styles include rock, blues, jazz, metal, country, and funk. Techniques taught include alternate picking, arpeggios, sweep picking, string skipping, legato, string bending, and rhythm guitar. These exercises will increase speed, and improve dexterity and pick- and fret-hand accuracy. The accompanying CD includes all 365 workout licks plus play-along grooves in every style at eight different metronome settings.
00695946 Book/CD Pack.........................$19.99

GUITAR CLUES
INCLUDES TAB

OPERATION PENTATONIC
by Greg Koch
Join renowned guitar master Greg Koch as he clues you in to a wide variety of fun and valuable pentatonic scale applications. Whether you're new to improvising or have been doing it for a while, this book/CD pack will provide loads of delicious licks and tricks that you can use right away, from volume swells and chicken pickin' to intervallic and chordal ideas. The CD includes 65 demo and play-along tracks.
00695827 Book/CD Pack.........................$19.95

INTRODUCTION TO GUITAR TONE & EFFECTS

by David M. Brewster
This book/CD pack teaches the basics of guitar tones and effects, with audio examples on CD. Readers will learn about: overdrive, distortion and fuzz • using equalizers • modulation effects • reverb and delay • multi-effect processors • and more.
00695766 Book/CD Pack.........................$14.95

PICTURE CHORD ENCYCLOPEDIA

This comprehensive guitar chord resource for all playing styles and levels features five voicings of 44 chord qualities for all twelve keys – 2,640 chords in all! For each, there is a clearly illustrated chord frame, as well as *an actual photo* of the chord being played! Includes info on basic fingering principles, open chords and barre chords, partial chords and broken-set forms, and more.
00695224.........................$19.95

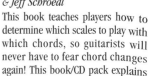

SCALE CHORD RELATIONSHIPS
INCLUDES TAB

by Michael Mueller & Jeff Schroedl
This book teaches players how to determine which scales to play with which chords, so guitarists will never have to fear chord changes again! This book/CD pack explains how to: recognize keys • analyze chord progressions • use the modes • play over nondiatonic harmony • use harmonic and melodic minor scales • use symmetrical scales such as chromatic, whole-tone and diminished scales • incorporate exotic scales such as Hungarian major and Gypsy minor • and much more!
00695563 Book/CD Pack.........................$14.95

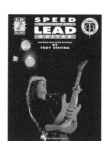

SPEED MECHANICS FOR LEAD GUITAR
INCLUDES TAB

Take your playing to the stratosphere with the most advanced lead book by this proven heavy metal author. *Speed Mechanics* is the ultimate technique book for developing the kind of speed and precision in today's explosive playing styles. Learn the fastest ways to achieve speed and control, secrets to make your practice time really count, and how to open your ears and make your musical ideas more solid and tangible. Packed with over 200 vicious exercises including Troy's scorching version of "Flight of the Bumblebee." Music and examples demonstrated on CD. 89-minute audio.
00699323 Book/CD Pack.........................$19.95

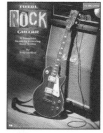

TOTAL ROCK GUITAR
INCLUDES TAB

A COMPLETE GUIDE TO LEARNING ROCK GUITAR
by Troy Stetina
This unique and comprehensive source for learning rock guitar is designed to develop both lead and rhythm playing. It covers: getting a tone that rocks • open chords, power chords and barre chords • riffs, scales and licks • string bending, strumming, palm muting, harmonics and alternate picking • all rock styles • and much more. The examples are in standard notation with chord grids and tab, and the CD includes full-band backing for all 22 songs.
00695246 Book/CD Pack.........................$19.99